I AM SCOUT

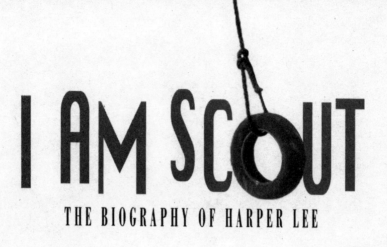

I AM SCOUT

THE BIOGRAPHY OF HARPER LEE

CHARLES J. SHIELDS

SQUARE
FISH

Henry Holt and Company • New York

SQUARE FISH

An Imprint of Macmillan
175 Fifth Avenue
New York, NY 10010
mackids.com

Square Fish and the Square Fish logo are trademarks of Macmillan and are used by
Henry Holt and Company, LLC under license from Macmillan.

Square Fish books may be purchased for business or promotional use. For information
on bulk purchases, please contact the Macmillan Corporate and Premium Sales
Department at (800) 221-7945 x5442 or by e-mail at specialmarkets@macmillan.com.

Library of Congress Cataloging-in-Publication Data
Shields, Charles J.
I am Scout : the biography of Harper Lee / Charles J. Shields.
p.   cm.
Includes bibliographical references and index.
ISBN 978-1-250-08221-3 (paperback) / ISBN 978-1-4668-6752-9 (ebook)
1. Lee, Harper—Juvenile literature. 2. Authors, American—20th century—
Biography—Juvenile literature. I. Title.
PS3562.E353Z85 2008
813'.54—dc22   [B]   2007027572

Originally published in the United States by Henry Holt and Company, LLC
First Square Fish Edition: 2015
Book designed by Barbara Grzeslo
Square Fish logo designed by Filomena Tuosto

10 9 8 7 6 5 4 3 2 1

AR: 8.3 / LEXILE: 1120L

To my wife, Guadalupe

Contents

A Note from the Author

Why is Harper Lee's *To Kill a Mockingbird* still talked about and read? Why would a novel set in a Southern town a long time ago, where the kids tease a weird neighbor, and the hero loses an unfair court case, still interest anyone? Sounds gloomy. And about mean people, too.

Well, there will always be a place on people's bookshelves for a really good story. And *To Kill a Mockingbird* is exactly that—funny in places, scary in others, and full of action with characters we want to know. Harper Lee's novel is a page-turner—right through to the end with a murder on Halloween night.

Second, novels that live on tend to treat fears that people struggle with: What would it be like to be poor, or unloved, or different, or criticized for trying to do what's right? Nearly everyone has experienced some of these issues, and finding out how the characters in *To Kill a Mockingbird* handle them keeps readers coming back.

Finally, a good book reads you as you read it. In other words, you care about the decisions the characters have to make. You wonder, "What would I do?"

As you read about the Tom Robinson rape case, for instance, you might wonder, "Would I stand up to the whole town like Atticus, knowing I was going to lose?" Or as Scout, Jem, and Dill work out the mystery of Boo Radley—raw-squirrel eater—you might wish you could join in, or you might think, "Leave him alone! How would you like it?" Strong pieces of fiction such as *To Kill a Mockingbird* force us to admit what actually matters to us, and therefore to admit who we are.

I wrote *I Am Scout* to help young readers learn more about Harper Lee and her much-loved novel. And now there is a second book from her desk: *Go Set a Watchman,* written a few years before *To Kill a Mockingbird* but published fifty-five years after! The title refers to Atticus as the self-appointed watchman outside the county jail, waiting for the mob to show up. He's the conscience of the town, the symbol of United States law and the Constitution. All of that invested in one, humble country lawyer.

Heroes come from all walks of life. Maybe some steps you decide to take today will start your journey in that direction, too.

—Charles J. Shields
Charlottesville, Virginia
February 23, 2015

Chapter 1

"Ellen" Spelled Backward

"GET *OFFA* HIM!" NELLE ROARED. "GET OFF NOW!"

Though she was only seven years old in 1933, Nelle Harper Lee peeled the older boys away from her friend and next-door neighbor Truman Streckfus Persons. He was lying on his back, red-faced and tearful, in the sandpit of the Monroe County Elementary School playground in Monroeville, Alabama. The bigger boys had been playing a game called Hot Grease in the Kitchen, Go Around! With their arms crossed, they dared anyone to try to get past them and into the sandpit.

But Truman, who adored attention, couldn't resist. He had marched directly toward the older boys and forced his way through. What he didn't expect was how furiously they would attack him. Shouts and flailing fists assaulted him, until Nelle barged into the circle and pulled him to his feet. Then she shoved past the angry boys and escorted her injured friend away, glancing over her shoulder to make sure she and Truman weren't being followed.[1]

But most boys knew better than to try that. Nelle had a

reputation as a fearsome stomach-puncher, foot-stomper, and hair-puller, who "could talk mean like a boy."[2] Three boys had tried challenging her once. They came at her, one at a time, bravely galloping toward a dragon. Within moments, each had landed facedown, spitting gravel and crying "Uncle!"

She was "a sawed-off but solid tomboy with an all-hell-let-loose wrestling technique," wrote Truman of a short story character he later based on Nelle.[3] Girls tended to be wary around her, too. During a game of softball, Nelle slammed into the girl playing first base, bowling her over and ripping her dress. "I was not fond of Nelle," said the former ballplayer, thinking back on that collision years later. "She was a bully, thought she knew so much more than anybody else, and probably did."[4]

Bully was a word often used to describe Nelle, but it can also be seen as an envious compliment. She was a fighter on the playground and frightened those who wouldn't stand up for themselves. She relied on herself and was independent, giving the impression at times that she was snobbish. And because she didn't try to conceal how smart and curious she was, she defied rules of good behavior for children. A fourth-grade classmate watched "in awe when Nelle would 'talk back' to the teachers. She was strong-willed and outspoken."[5] When she called her teacher, Mrs. McNeil, by her first name "Leighton," Mrs. McNeil was shocked. But why? Nelle wanted to know. She called her father by *his* first name! It was typical of how Nelle went her own way most of the time. Her eldest sister, Alice, 15 years older, later admitted that her little sister, the youngest of four children, "isn't much of a conformist."[6]

It was true she was tough and independent. She preferred wearing a scruffy pair of overalls to a dress and hanging upside down from the chinaberry tree in her yard to sitting quietly in a church. But actually, her folks were upper-middle class. Her home life was the product of several generations of southern Alabama farmers raising themselves up from hardship.

The Lees had long been Deep South Southerners. Nelle's father was the son of a Civil War veteran, Cader Alexander Lee, a private who fought in 22 battles with the 15th Alabama Regiment. (Her family is not related to Confederate general Robert E. Lee, as encyclopedias claim.)[7] After the South surrendered at Appomattox Courthouse in Virginia in April 1865, Cader Lee, 26, did his best to steer his life back on course. On September 6, 1866, he married 22-year-old Theodocia Eufrassa Windham, a sister of a distant cousin killed during the war. Less than two years later, the first of their nine children was born. In the middle of the brood, Amasa Coleman Lee, Harper Lee's father, was born July 19, 1880, in Georgiana, a village in Butler County, Alabama, 60 miles south of Montgomery. His family nicknamed him "Coley." Within a few years, they moved to northern Florida.

Coley Lee's upbringing took place in a "staunch Methodist home," he recalled, meaning his parents frowned on drinking, card playing, and other time-wasting behavior. On Sundays, his father hitched up the horses for a three-and-a-half-mile trip from their farm in Chipley, Florida, to services at the local Methodist church. The message of those sermons became the central philosophy of his life: salvation through believing in the gospel of Jesus was only the first step in fulfilling a responsibility to help reform humanity. Years later, as a civic leader in Monroeville and an Alabama state legislator, Nelle's father was a strong believer in the need to uplift people. "Progress," he argued, "might be defined as any activity which brings the greatest possible number of benefits to the greatest possible number of people."[8]

Even after Coley reached the age for regular schooling, chores on the farm took precedence over schoolwork. Some winter evenings he ran out of daylight before he could finish his lessons. But he was a steady reader, and at 16 he passed the examination to teach. For three years he taught school near Marianna, Florida.

Then, eager for better wages, he shook the dust of Florida from his heels. In southern Alabama, big sawmills were eating deep into the piney woods—one appearing every five miles or so along railroad tracks, filling the air with the scream of buzz saws and the vinegary smell of fresh lumber. Mills employed 50 to 80 men, about one third of them black, and there was plenty of work for laborers. But Coley—introducing himself as "A. C. Lee" now—was a whiz at numbers and landed a job as a bookkeeper. Over the next several years, a series of better-paying positions followed. Finally, he found work at the Flat Creek Mill in Finchburg, Alabama, a tiny town named after the postmaster, James Finch. Then one day at church, A.C. met Finch's 19-year-old daughter, Frances Cunningham Finch.

———

Frances's father was a farmer and part-time postmaster. Her mother, Ellen C. Finch (her maiden name was Williams), came from money: her family owned a plantation in southwest Alabama. The land was excellent, bordered as it was by the Alabama River, then rising into high fields above the flood-plains. Steamboats arrived to off-load goods and take on the Williamses' cotton, raised and picked by slaves. It was one of many real-life places and people that Nelle later drew on when she came to write *To Kill a Mockingbird*. "Finch's Landing," as she renamed the Williamses' plantation in the novel, "produced everything required to sustain life except ice, wheat flour, and articles of clothing, supplied by river-boats from Mobile."[9] Although James Finch and his wife were not as well-off as their in-laws, they gave their children the best education they could afford.

When their daughters Frances and Alice each reached 15, the Finches enrolled them in the new Alabama Girls' Industrial School in Montevallo, a progressive institution for white girls. In today's terms, it resembled a private college prep school. The students studied English, Latin, history, and mathematics. In addition, they could choose from vocational electives, including stenography; photography; typewriting; printing; bookkeeping; indoor carpentry; electrical construction; clay modeling; architectural and mechanical drawing; sewing; dress-making; cooking; laundering; sign and fresco painting; home nursing; and "other practical industries."[10] The curriculum guaranteed that graduates could make their own way in the world.

To keep the focus on academics, the girls wore uniforms: a navy blue dress and cap trimmed with white cord and a tassel. Trips off campus required a chaperone because, as the school catalog warned, "pupils are not here to enter society, but to be educated"; furthermore, "they are not allowed to correspond with gentlemen, and visits from them is positively prohibited under penalty of expulsion."[11]

The Finches were wholeheartedly in favor of this no-nonsense curriculum for cultivating young women. And so when A. C. Lee entered the picture—a self-made, self-educated young man who was preparing himself for bigger things—they recognized a good match for their daughter. And Frances—an artistic, some might say pampered young woman—had every reason to expect the kind of genteel life she had been educated for.

The couple married on June 22, 1910. A.C. was 30 years old, and Frances, 19. During the ensuing years, the Lees would have four children: Alice (1911); Frances Louise (1916); and Edwin (1920). When their youngest child, Nelle, was born on April 28, 1926, her parents gave her the first name of her maternal grandmother, Ellen Finch, spelled backward.

———

In 1912, two years after their marriage, the Lees moved with one-year-old Alice to Nelle's future birthplace, Monroeville, 15 miles southeast of Finchburg where the couple had met. For 80 years, since its founding as the county seat of Monroe County in 1832, Monroeville had been snoozing in the muggy breezes from the Gulf of Mexico, a pretty sad spectacle.

The reason Monroeville had failed to flourish was that it was a poor choice for the county seat in the first place. Everything and everybody had to rattle into town overland because there were no rivers or railroads nearby. By 1860, the population of Monroeville teetered at about 300—half white and half black. A Confederate soldier passing through town in the mid-1860s, during the Civil War, described it as "the most boring place in the world."[12] Forty years later, in 1900, there were still no paved streets or sidewalks and no street lights. Houses and other buildings were unpainted; and churches and schools looked dilapidated.

But in 1912, when the Lees arrived in Monroeville, the town was finally ready to prosper. A sign of progress rumbled and whistled its way into town that year, when the first locomotive of the Manistee & Repton Railroad arrived on freshly laid tracks. In fact, the new railroad was the reason the Lees had moved to Monroeville. Mr. Lee had been newly hired as financial manager with the law firm of Barnett, Bugg & Jones, handling their interests in the Manistee & Repton. The M&R, as local people called it, began hauling freight and passengers east from Monroeville to Manistee Junction, where it joined the mighty Louisville & Nashville Railroad.

The benefits to Monroeville of the railroad's arrival were staggering. After 1912, brick structures began replacing old weather-beaten wooden buildings, giving the town the appearance of real permanence. Although Monroeville's economy was based on only a handful of humble but necessary industries—a sawmill, a cotton ginnery, a gristmill, a fertilizer plant, a machine shop, lumberyard, and a waterworks plant—an enormous new high school opened the same year the railroad arrived, indicating that a better future lay ahead for Monroeville's young people.

A.C.'s career prospered in the offices of Barnett, Bugg &

Jones. First, he served as the financial manager; then, by "reading for the law," as it was called—a kind of home-schooling under the guidance of attorneys—he passed the bar examination in 1915.

Plenty of legal cases would likely come his way, as Monroeville was the county seat. The enormous white-domed courthouse, built in 1903 in the center of the town square, was "one

As a young attorney, A. C. Lee was appointed in 1919 to defend two blacks accused of murdering a white man. He lost; they both were hanged. (History of Alabama and Her People, 1927; photographer unidentified)

of the handsomest and most conveniently appointed in the state," boasted the *Monroe Journal,* "and one that would do credit to a county far exceeding Monroe in wealth and population."[13] From the corridors of the courthouse, all the administrators and servants of county government spent every weekday issuing a paper stream of court orders, motions, certificates, writs, deeds, wills, plats, bills of sale, affidavits, and depositions. As Scout says about Maycomb, the fictional town based on Monroeville, in *To Kill a Mockingbird,* "Because its primary reason for existence was government, Maycomb was spared the grubbiness that distinguished most Alabama towns its size."[14]

Steadily A. C. Lee was ascending the rungs of respectability: from teacher in a country school, to bookkeeper, to financial manager, to attorney.

———

Despite outward signs that the Lees were doing well, many people thought there was something a little odd about them. Mr. and Mrs. Lee were educated people, and their children—Alice, Louise, Edwin, and Nelle—were known to be bright and friendly. What seemed peculiar about the Lees were signs that the family was coping with problems at home.

To begin with, any thoughtful person could see that A. C. Lee tended to keep himself in check. He stuck to routines and was methodical and reserved. He often gave the impression of having something heavy on his mind.

"Mr. Lee was detached," Truman's aunt Marie recalled, "not particularly friendly, especially with children. . . . He was not the sort of father who came up to his children, ruffled their hair, and made jokes for their amusement."[15] In Mr. Lee's presence, said an acquaintance, "you didn't feel comfortable with him. But that he was nice."[16]

Part of his standoffishness around children may have been that he was already in his 50s when Nelle was in first grade. (In *To Kill a Mockingbird*, Scout says about her father, "When Jem and I asked him why he was so old, he said he got started late, which we felt reflected on his abilities and his manliness.")[17]

Of course, some of his reserve may also have been rooted in Southern manners, too. Doctors, lawyers, teachers— professional people in general—were expected to behave in a courteous but authoritative way. They were educated, and therefore acknowledged leaders in the community. Said the son of a businessman who golfed with A. C. Lee for years, "I doubt they ever called each other by first names. Those were different times."[18]

Seen up close, A. C. Lee was of average height and weight, with a flat, serious face and mild expression. Behind a pair of large, round glasses, his thoughtful gaze looked owlish. Every weekday morning, he would walk down the steps of his wood-frame white one-story bungalow on South Alabama Avenue on his way to his law offices above the bank in the town square. He did not greet passersby on the street with a hearty "good morning." If the weather was rainy, Mr. Lee drove his black Chevrolet. He was a Chevy man his entire life, not given to flashiness even though he was one of the wealthiest men in town.

He wore a dark three-piece suit that sagged and lost its crease in the Alabama heat during the summertime. He always wore a suit, everywhere, even when golfing and the only time anyone could recall him hunting. That day he trudged around under the trees and shot a few doves—almost as a favor to the friend who had invited him—then he went straight back to the office. He wasn't much interested in that sort of thing. One of his former golf caddies remembered Mr. Lee as "much more of an intellectual than a physical man. The image of shooting the mad dog or of facing down the crowd of rough necks [as Atticus Finch does] has never quite rung true to me. The strong intellectual stand, though, seems very natural."[19]

When he was lost in thought he had a habit of absentmindedly fumbling with things, including his watch, a fountain pen, or his special favorite: a tiny pocketknife. He flipped it up with his thumb and caught it like a coin while he talked. Once, a store clerk waited while Mr. Lee practiced flipping different penknives until he found one with exactly the right weight and balance. "He could hold it between two fingers and thump it in a way that it would just spin around," recalled Charles Skinner, a friend of Nelle's older brother, Edwin. "He'd stand there and talk to you—he wouldn't look at the knife, he'd just thump it around. And it would just be whirling around in his hand. It was an automatic thing with him, I don't think he ever knew what he was doing."[20]

In addition to playing with objects while he spoke, his manner of speaking was slow and careful. He did not make conversation as much as let fall a comment that usually began with "ah-hem!" contained "uh," and sometimes, for emphasis, ended with "ah-rum!"[21] Generally, he preferred listening to talking, while sucking on a piece of hard candy.

Even on social occasions, he was never one to cut loose. He never accepted a drink or offered to pay for one. A. C. Lee, everyone in town knew, was a strict Methodist, and when it came to liquor, he was "dry as an old sun-bleached bone."[22]

At the Monroeville Methodist Episcopal Church, where he was a deacon, congregation members noted that he usually sat near the front by himself, preferring to be alone with his thoughts. When it was time to pray, he would rise, face the congregation, and deliver a long improvised prayer, tapping out a rhythm for his rumbling voice on the pew with his penknife.

———

Why Mr. Lee seemed so distant only some of the neighbors on South Alabama Avenue and a handful of close friends understood. He was serious by nature, it was true, but he was also preoccupied with worries—mainly about his wife and her mental health. To outsiders, that would have been a surprise, because on the surface at least, Mrs. Lee appeared to be a contented housewife married to a successful attorney.

Most days at about 10:00 A.M., she appeared on the porch of the white bungalow to water her flower boxes. She was a large woman but carried herself gracefully and preferred simple cotton prints. She made the most of her best feature—thick, platinum blond hair—by wearing it braided and coiled on the crown of her head. After pinching off dead flower blossoms or cutting back stems that had become too leggy, she went back inside, letting the screen door bang shut. In a few moments, piano music could be heard drifting from the front room. Her gift as a classical pianist had been one of the centerpieces of the orchestra at the Alabama Girls' Industrial School. In Monroeville, she was in demand as a performer at weddings, and she played at the wedding of Truman's parents. If the house remained quiet after she had gone inside, it meant she was probably working a crossword puzzle or reading. She was a "brilliant woman," Truman said; "she could do a *New York Times* crossword puzzle as fast as she could move a pencil, that kind of person."[23]

To minimize housework, she kept her home simple: there were no rugs to vacuum or shake out, the chairs were cane-backed, and the iron bedsteads had been painted white. The pine floors gleamed from regular polishing.[24] She had house-keepers—there was always one black woman, sometimes two, who cooked, cleaned, and looked after the children. They walked from a black neighborhood where they lived to the Lee home about a quarter mile away. Hattie Clausell lived in with the Lees for many years, and when Nelle came in after a day of play, sunburned and grass-stained, it was usually Hattie who ordered "Miss Frippy Britches" out of her hand-me-down overalls, to be scrubbed in the tub, combed, and given supper in the kitchen.[25] In fact, Hattie may have been the person Harper Lee was thinking about when she created Calpurnia.

In those days it was commonplace for middle- and upper-middle-class Southern white families to employ black house-keepers, cooks, or handymen. Carson McCullers, author of *The Member of the Wedding* and other novels, grew up in Georgia in the 1930s. Her home life was similar to Harper Lee's. "We knew 'colored people' as servants," said McCullers's cousin Roberta Steiner. "In both our houses we had a 'cook' who was really a general housekeeper. About half her time was spent with the baby if there was one. She did whatever was necessary at the time. We had a 'yard man' who came about once a week. Our clothes were picked up by a black woman with a wagon. She took them home, boiled them on an outside fire, starched them, ironed them and returned them. Sheets, etc., went to the commercial laundry. Extra help came in for fall cleaning. It was the way of life."26

Consequently, in *To Kill a Mockingbird*, the round-the-clock presence of Calpurnia is true-to-life. Although now we wonder how Calpurnia cared for her own family when she was looking after the Finch children.

———

Yet despite the extra help with running her home, and the comfort of four children who loved her, Mrs. Lee was an unhappy person. Part of the reason had to do with her circumstances. Life in a small town couldn't offer much to a woman of her talents and interests. She and Mr. Lee enjoyed books and music, but cultural activities were almost nonexistent. The standard of living in the South at the end of the 1920s was already the lowest in the nation. It was at the bottom of the list in almost everything: ownership of automobiles, radios, residential telephones; income per capita; bank deposits; homes with electricity, running water, and indoor plumbing. Southerners subscribed to the fewest magazines and newspapers and read the fewest books; they also provided the least support for education, public libraries, and art museums.27 Then the stock market crash of 1929 and the decade of the Great Depression that followed wiped out pastimes like book clubs, theater and musical performances, and other self-improvement activities. Church programs and ladies' charity work were practically the only opportunities available to someone with a lively mind like Mrs. Lee. The image of Mrs. Lee, a "brilliant woman," killing time by playing the piano for hours or reading is a sad portrait of a creative person with no outlet.

More serious, however, was Mrs. Lee's mental state. From the time Nelle was small, she knew her mother mainly as a middle-aged, overweight woman with a host of demons. Today her condition would probably be diagnosed as manic-depression, an emotional disorder involving severe mood swings and irrational thoughts. Her unpredictable behavior, over which she had little control, affected everyone in her family.

The "gentle soul" of the household, as her children later called her, could become inexplicably upset and tearful, or unaccountably talkative. Some days, Mrs. Lee "seemed withdrawn": she might remain blank-faced in response to a greeting, as if she had never seen the person before, or only nod in reply. On days when Mrs. Lee was too depressed to fix meals and Hattie or the cook couldn't come, the family settled for eating hunks of watermelon all day.[28]

Other times, her mood would veer to the opposite pole—her mind racing, words tumbling out. She would seize on a small piece of gossip, or something she'd heard on the radio, and exaggerate it beyond belief. From the porch, she would shout instructions to passersby on the street.[29] Bafflement in the Lee family over Mother's behavior reached its highest pitch when she would rise in the dead of night and begin playing the piano.

It was then that Mr. Lee had to coax her back to bed with the promise that she should rest and then play as much as she liked the following day. Eventually, Mr. Lee arranged for her to spend a few restful weeks at a beach resort on the Gulf of Mexico during the summer months, under the watchful eye of his secretary, Maggie Dees.

The Lees coped with Mrs. Lee's "nervous disorder," as they preferred to call it, as best they could. Alice, the eldest child, shifted some of her father's burdens onto herself by acting as his substitute helpmate in practical affairs. Her nickname in the family, interestingly, was "Bear." Louise, called "Weezie" by her siblings, concentrated on an active social life and swept problems at home into the background. Edwin, a natural athlete who stuck close to a few good friends, kept out of the way and was simply called "Brother." Nelle (pronounced Nel), the baby sister, was "Dody," for reasons known only to her family.

Mr. Lee responded to his wife's maladies and their effect on his family without complaint, probably reasoning that everybody had some kind of difficulty in life and on the whole he had much to be grateful for. But, Truman's aunt Marie observed, "I don't believe Mr. and Mrs. Lee were happy."[30]

———

Watching all this through a child's eye, Truman thought Mr. Lee was "wonderful"—A. C. Lee presented him with a pocket dictionary he cherished for years—but Nelle's mother, he said later, was an "eccentric character" and an "endless gossip." When he was in the sixth grade, he made fun of her in his first known short story, "Old Mrs. Busybody."

According to Truman, he submitted the story to the *Mobile Register* for a children's writing contest. "There was a children's page with contests for writing and for coloring pictures, and then every Saturday afternoon they had a party with free Nehi and Coca-Cola. The prize for the short-story writing contest was either a pony or a dog, I've forgotten which, but I wanted it badly." He said that when the story appeared in the newspaper, he instantly became a notorious character on South Alabama Avenue. "I'd walk down the street and people on their front porches would pause, fanning for a moment. I found they were very upset about it. I was a little hesitant about showing anything after that. I remember I said, 'Oh, I don't know why I did that, I've given up writing.' But I was writing more fiercely than ever."[31]

Truman was prone to telling lies (a trait of his that people learned the hard way) and it turns out he only submitted his story about Mrs. Lee as a school assignment. But one wonders if Nelle ever saw a version of her mother through her friend's eyes: "Mrs. Busybody was a fat old widow whose only amusement was crocheting and sewing. She was also fond of knitting. She didn't like the movies and took an immediate dislike to anyone who did enjoy them. She also took great delight in reporting children to their mothers over the slightest thing that annoyed her. In other words no one liked her and she was considered a public nuisance and a regular old Busybody."[32] Over the next 27 pages of Truman's lengthy story, written in pencil, Mrs. Busybody puts up with a visit from her atrocious in-laws—they fight, drink, and make jokes in poor taste—until they leave on the train for their home in "Slumtown." It was exactly the kind of situation that Mrs. Lee, raised in a polite girls' school environment, would have found extremely embarrassing.

If he dared show or describe "Old Mrs. Busybody" to Nelle, it probably would have been her first exposure to what writers learn over time: write about what you know. If people were hurt by it, as Truman claimed, Nelle also might have taken away a second lesson: lack of sympathy in a writer is a fault.

———

Because her parents were so different from each other—Mr. Lee, a man of business and outward-looking; Mrs. Lee, a reclusive and emotionally unstable woman—it's interesting to speculate about the kind of impact they might have had on Nelle.

She adored her father, that much we know. Although Mr. Lee's formality could be intimidating—a young businessman in the Rotary Club said he could never bring himself to call Mr. Lee "Coley," even though Lee invited him to—he was an understanding father. Nelle often dropped into his offices for a visit. At home, she would climb into his lap to read the newspaper with him or help fill in the squares of crosswords. A playmate couldn't believe his ears when Nelle called her father "A.C.," the way adults did.[33] Apparently, Mr. Lee's attitudes toward child raising were similar to that of the hero of Nelle's novel, Atticus Finch. He spoke to his children in an adultlike manner, extending them the privilege to think and reply like grown-ups. They loved him for this mark of respect.

But Frances Lee's "nervous disorder" made her less approachable as a parent. Eventually, as her disturbances grew worse, and neighbors began speaking about her suffering from "hardening of the arteries" and "second childhood"—common expressions for mental illness in adults back then—Mr. Lee took her to hospitals in nearby cities for treatments. Nelle, watching her mother decline over the years, would naturally have felt more secure with her father.

She probably chose him for her role model, too. After all, he was independent and influential. The moment he stepped off the front porch and headed for the town square, he was fulfilling a destiny of his own choosing. Mrs. Lee, on the other hand, was trapped in a situation unsuited to her abilities. In fact, as Mrs. Lee's condition deteriorated, she became a virtual prisoner inside her house. Despite having the amenities of an upper-middle-class home—a phonograph to play her favorite symphonies and a piano to practice all day if she wished—she was deeply and perhaps even dangerously unhappy there. After a while, "she was kept on the premises," according to Truman's aunt Marie because she couldn't be trusted to go to Monroeville's town square alone.[34]

So if Nelle—the tomboy, the roughhouser—resisted the normal expectations for her gender, perhaps it's because they seemed too limiting. "She was just like a boy!" enthused Taylor Faircloth, a resident of Atmore, Alabama, where Nelle spent summers visiting her mother's sister, Aunt Alice McKinley. "She would come down and stay sometimes three or four weeks in the summer. . . . She got rid of all her surplus hair in the summertime, and she could climb tall trees. When we played 'capture the flag' at night, she held on longer than anybody!"[35]

In the same ways, Scout expresses disdain for activities girls were expected to like: "Aunt Alexandra's vision of my deportment involved playing with small stoves, tea sets, and wearing the Add-A-Pearl necklace she gave me when I was born," she complains in the novel.[36]

Yet there may be one more reason, a dark one, why Nelle identified more with her father than with her mother: a pair of incidents that allegedly happened when she was a toddler that may have snapped the bond between mother and daughter forever. According to Truman, Mrs. Lee, during one of her emotional fits, twice tried to drown Nelle in the bathtub when she was two years old.[37] An acquaintance of the family said Nelle's older sisters, Louise and Alice, ran into the bathroom screaming and saved her.

Alice, when she heard Truman's remarks repeated on a popular radio program years later, angrily issued a public statement calling them "a pack of lies."[38]

But when Nelle created Scout and gave her a voice, her pen seems to have wandered back to that incident: "Our mother died when I was two," Scout says, "so I never felt her absence."[39] The coincidence of Mrs. Finch dying when Scout was two and the supposed attempted drowning when Nelle was two might explain why there is no mother in *To Kill a Mockingbird*. In her fiction at least, Nelle wiped the slate clean of her emotional conflict with her mother.

Only in Aunt Alexandra, the sole adult female member of the immediate Finch family, is there a possible suggestion as to how Nelle saw her mother: "Aunt Alexandra was one of the last of her kind: she had river-boat, boarding-school manners;

let any moral come along and she would uphold it; she was born in the objective case; she was an incurable gossip. . . . Had I ever harbored the mystical notions about mountains that seem to obsess lawyers and judges, Aunt Alexandra would have been analogous to Mount Everest: throughout my early life, she was cold and there."[40]

Chapter 2

"Apart People"

N ELLE WAS GOING ON FIVE YEARS OLD THE SUMMER OF
1930, when she began playing with Truman; he was almost
six. "Beautiful things floated around in his dreamy head," she
would later write of him, when he became Dill, the lonely boy
next door in *To Kill a Mockingbird*.[1]

Whatever his imaginative gifts, however, at first glance
Truman hardly seemed the ideal candidate for friendship with
a girl like Nelle. She was a female Huck Finn, with large
dark brown eyes and close-cropped hair. Whereas he—as surely
as every child at Monroe County Elementary knew that night
followed day—was a sissy, a crybaby, a mamma's boy, and
so on.

To begin with, his clothes made him a target for other children's ridicule. It was the 1930s, the Great Depression, when
children went to school in hand-me-downs that had been
patched and altered several times. A girl wearing a cotton dress
carefully cut and sewn from a 50-pound flour sack had nothing
to feel ashamed of. Many children came to school without

shoes, their dirty heels thumping on the pine floors. So when Truman's cousin Jennie, with whom he lived, outfitted him in Hawaiian shirts, white duck shorts, blue socks, sandals, and Eton caps from the best department stores in Mobile and Montgomery, he looked, as one teacher expressed it, "like a bird of paradise among a flock of crows."[2] The implied insult to the other children could not be ignored. Boys socked him and rubbed cockleburs into his fine blond hair.

In addition, he was undersized, which he could do nothing about. Compared with his classmates, he was the smallest by far—doll-like, with a baby's pudgy gumdrop softness. Even Nelle, who was younger, "was bigger than Truman. Lots bigger," said another of Truman's aunts, Mary Ida Carter.[3]

And much to other children's disgust, Truman threw tantrums like a two-year-old. In the throes of one, he would scream until he turned purple, fall down, and kick his legs in the air. No amount of cooing, patting, or hugging could calm him until his rage had passed.

The adults in his life knew the reason for his flare-ups. He would go almost insane with anger because the worst thing that could happen to any child had happened to him. His parents didn't want him. Worse, they didn't mind if he knew it, either.

Truman's mother, Lillie Mae, a "rare beauty" in Monroeville, and his father, Archilus Julius Persons, a hustler and disbarred attorney, dumped their only child with his cousins, the Faulks—three single ladies and their bachelor brother, all middle-aged and elderly—who lived next door to the Lees. Freed from the burdens of parenthood, Arch had sped away in a rented, chauffeured limousine in pursuit of get-rich-quick schemes, while Lillie Mae had flown to New York to live the high life. A "discontented small-town beauty," Lillie Mae "would appear in [Truman's] life for a day or two," wrote a journalist describing Truman's childhood, "wafting the perfume of motherhood over him, then disappear."[4] Once, out of desperation, Truman drank a bottle of his mother's perfume to try to make her part of him.[5]

Considering the differences between Truman and Nelle— "he was too soft for the boys, and she was too rough for the girls," as a neighbor boy later remarked—the chances of their becoming friends seemed far-fetched.[6] He was "shrimp-o," and "that funny boy," and sometimes "Bulldog," because, added to everything else, he had an underbite that gave him a Halloween pumpkin grin. Nelle, on the other hand, had "fire in those big brown eyes as they stared dead ahead," recalled a classmate after watching her win another fight with boys.[7]

But Nelle took on Truman as her closest playmate, and he followed her around the school playground like a little fish swimming in her wake. At home on South Alabama Avenue, they raced to play with each other. Truman's aunt Marie recalled seeing them climb into the tree house on Nelle's property, or bent over a game on the sidewalk. Nelle was best at shooting marbles. Truman excelled at swiping jacks off the sidewalk so fast that his hand was a blur.

They fought, too, of course. As a friend, Truman could be a handful. Throughout his life he would test the devotion of those who tried to care for him, Nelle included. But she wouldn't let him get under her skin, even when he marred a nice afternoon spent cutting out magazine pictures by raging at her.

"Stop that, Nelle. Keep your hands off my pictures. I hate you, Nelle. I really do."

"You shut up, you silly little shrimp, or I'll knock your silly block off."[8]

He couldn't push her far.

When his rages failed, he tried shaming her into letting him have his way by playing the victim. He pulled tantrums on her. But she had older siblings and didn't have an only child's expectation of special treatment. In response to his bawling she would hurl him to the ground as if to demonstrate that crybabies were losers.

"She was tough on me," Truman later said.[9]

Yet despite their spats and grudging reconciliations, the two friends remained inseparable. They swam in the pond at Rickard's Mill, in Beatrice, where fish tickled their legs. Sometimes they hiked the dirt road that led to the farm of Truman's cousin Jennings, whom Truman nicknamed "Big Boy," even though he wasn't much older than Truman. Jennings's mother, Aunt Mary Ida, welcomed them with homemade biscuits, jam, butter, and fresh milk. Although Truman "felt like a turtle on its back" in Monroeville, he could count on Nelle as his steadfast friend there.[10] Her faithfulness was something she never hesitated to prove.

The secret of their closeness was mysterious to others, but they understood it. Besides liking each other, Nelle later referred to their bond as sharing a "common anguish."[11]

———

A look at each of their family lives suggests why. It's likely that Nelle, as a daughter, and Truman, as a son, were not their mothers' ideals in those roles. After all, deliberately or not, Nelle rebelled at what her mother valued. She would not go willingly into the "pink cotton penitentiary," as Scout calls it, of girlhood. The charms of Miss Tutwiler's Alabama Girls' Industrial School—dressmaking, cooking, and the like—would not have held her attention long. Nelle couldn't even accept her teachers' instructions without asking a slew of questions. Hence, Mrs. Lee and her stubborn daughter lived in two different worlds.

For his part, Truman fell short of his mother's hopes in a similar way. Lillie Mae thought a boy should be rough-and-tumble. He acted effeminate. And as he grew older, his mother openly resented this. "Lillie Mae continually attacked him for behavior she thought effeminate and improper," said Truman's aunt Marie. "She rode him constantly."[12] Truman's aunt claimed to have overheard his mother railing at him about his masculinity: " 'Truman, I swear, we give you every advantage, and you can't behave. If it were just failing out of school, I could take it. But, my God, why can't you be more like a normal boy your age? I mean—well, the whole thing about you is so obvious. I mean—you know what I mean. Don't take me for a fool.' " Actually, he was quick, agile, and determined. One of his best stunts was leaping up on the rock wall between his house and Nelle's and turning cartwheels. And he lived up to the nickname of Bulldog more than once by head-butting adversaries and knocking them down. A friend saw him do it in the lobby of the Lyric movie theater in Mobile, only that time Bulldog sailed in a bit low and hit the kid between the legs.[13]

In any case, both Nelle and Truman were not their mothers'

ideals. But there was little they could do about it. They were who they were. A "common anguish" based on failing to win approval from their mothers would have united them, but it would have been painful, too.

———

Truman had his own explanation for the bond between them. He said it was because they were "apart people."[14]

What he meant is captured by a glimpse of the two friends at the Strand movie theater in the town square one Saturday afternoon. According to a Monroe County Elementary School classmate who saw them, they were immersed in a game they had invented. One would spell a word, but leave out a few letters; the other would have to guess the complete word. While they were playing, kids were shouting, teasing, and noisily finding seats. Yet Nelle and Truman were concentrating so hard on their game that they were lost to anything else. "They were a little above the rest of the kids in town."[15]

In their defense, as bright children they turned to each other because there wasn't much else to do. There were no books to take home from school because it had none to loan. Pictures at the Strand movie theater tended to be Westerns, adventures, or romances, because people wanted to forget their problems for a few hours. In most households, the world funneled into the living room via radio or newspaper only.

Not even school offered an oasis for imaginative children. On the first day of first grade, Truman proudly recited the alphabet all the way through and got whacked on the palm by the teacher with a ruler.[16] Children weren't supposed to come to school knowing how to read. It was this incident, or a similar one involving Nelle, that inspired the scene in *To Kill a Mockingbird* when Scout complains to Jem about her first-grade teacher: "that damn lady says Atticus's been teaching me to read and for him to stop it."[17]

Looking back, Nelle summarized what her early years were like in a town that could offer little to stimulate the mind. "This was my childhood," Nelle said. "If I went to a film once a month it was pretty good for me, and for all children like me. We had to use our own devices in our play, for our entertainment. We didn't have much money. Nobody had any money. We didn't have toys, nothing was done for us, so the result was that we lived in our imaginations most of the time."[18]

One way "apart people" with time on their hands could feed their imaginations was to read. Truman's cousin Jennings recalled how Nelle and Truman's mutual love of reading created a bond that put them in splendid isolation.

"The year I began school Truman and Nelle were knee-deep reading Sherlock Holmes detective books. Even though I hadn't learned to read with their speed and comprehension, we three would climb up in Nelle's big tree house and curl up with books. Truman or Nelle would stop from time to time to read some interesting event aloud. We'd discuss what might happen next in the story and try to guess which character would be the culprit. Sometimes Truman called me 'Inspector.' Nelle was 'Dr. Watson.'"[19]

The *Rover Boys* was another favorite series, despite the stories' stiff dialogue—"'Hello, you fellows!' shouted a voice from behind the Rover boys. 'Plotting mischief?'" At least they featured a girlfriend-sidekick named Nellie.

Then, said Nelle, "As we grew older, we began to realize what our books were worth: *Anne of Green Gables* was worth two Bobbsey Twins; two *Rover Boys* were an even swap for two Tom Swifts. . . . The goal, a full set of a series, was attained only once by an individual of exceptional greed—he swapped his sister's doll buggy."[20]

———

Mr. Lee, seeing that Nelle and Truman had fallen in love with words, encouraged them with a special gift. When they were old enough to write stories of their own, he gave them a typewriter. It was the 1930s equivalent of a word processor: a rugged, steel-encased black Underwood No. 5.

Most children probably would have begun by creating original fairy tales. But an invasion of fairies in down-and-out Monroeville seemed far-fetched. Anyway, their favorite books featured real-life places. Why couldn't Monroeville—their neighborhood, in fact—do just as well as a setting? This would also fit with another of their favorite activities: people watching. They knew more about "Doc" Watson, the dentist, and his family who lived across the street, for instance, than they would ever know about trolls and so on.

As a result of this line of thinking, the residents of South Alabama Avenue unknowingly became characters in the first stories of Truman Streckfus Persons and Nelle Harper Lee, authors, one of whose earliest efforts (since lost) bore the interesting title "The Fire and the Flame."[21] One writer would dictate the story slowly while the other typed, and then they would switch places. Looking back, Nelle was of the opinion that small-town life "naturally produces more writers than, say, an environment like 82nd Street in New York. In small town life and in rural life you know your neighbors. Not only do you know everything about your neighbors, but you know everything about them from the time they came to the country."[22]

And there was certainly no lack of interesting people to cast as characters on South Alabama Avenue. At the top of the list were Truman's elderly cousins, the Faulks. Jennie Faulk had built the rambling, two-story house next door to the Lees as a shared dwelling for her three siblings: sister Callie, two years younger than she; brother Bud; and sister Sook, who, despite being white-haired, had the mind and personality of a 14-year-old girl. (Sook is the fruitcake-baking "aunt" portrayed in Truman's novelette *A Christmas Memory*.) She was rarely comfortable with anyone except children, and she drew Nelle, Truman, and Jennings to her. They spent many happy hours sitting at her feet being fed, like open-mouthed birds, cookies dipped in coffee, or they perched in her lap and made up long, fantastic tales.

To the south of the Faulks lived ex–Confederate Captain and Mrs. Powell Jones, whose house was best avoided. The Joneses were very old; Mrs. Jones, an invalid in a wheelchair, was addicted to a powerful pain-relieving drug called morphine. Neighbors heard her screeching at her husband about her medicine. Children passing by received a good dose of her unpleasantness, too. (Many Monroeville residents would later recognize Mrs. Jones as the model for Mrs. Dubose in *To Kill a Mockingbird*, who tormented Scout and Jem with her vicious taunts.)

But for sheer mystery and speculation, no source was richer

This cabin outside Monroeville in the 1930s is similar to the one Tom Robinson in To Kill a Mockingbird *would have lived in. (Library of Congress)*

Nelle's next-door neighbor Truman Capote, in the 1920s, with his elderly cousin Sook. "Beautiful things floated around in his dreamy head," Nelle would later write of Truman as Dill in To Kill a Mockingbird. *(Photographer unknown)*

than the tumbledown Boleware place just two doors south of the Lees', past Captain and Mrs. Powell Jones's place, its backyard flush against the playground of the elementary school. It was a dark, ramshackle structure with most of the paint fallen off. What went on inside was a matter of guesswork, because the shutters were always closed, as if the house were asleep. Children held their noses while walking by, or crossed to the other side of the street, to avoid inhaling evil vapors that might be steaming from cracks in the house's boards.

The owner was Alfred R. Boleware, 60, a merchant and a big man in town, but a know-it-all and cheapskate. He and his wife, Annie, had three children—Mary and Sally, both in their late 20s, and Alfred, Jr., a few years younger than his sisters, who was nicknamed "Son."[23]

Mr. Boleware wouldn't spend a dime on his house, or its raggedy yard of tangled pecan trees, broken scuppernong arbor, and weedy garden. But his sagging estate belonged to him, and no one was permitted to put a foot on it without his permission. A well-hit ball from the schoolyard that landed in the Bolewares' weeds might as well have rolled into a minefield. Everyone knew better than to retrieve it. When the pecans ripened and fell, old man Boleware stood in the backyard, arms crossed, as if daring any pipsqueak on the playground to risk life and limb by stealing one.

Adding to the mystery of the Boleware house was the legend of Son, who was said to be languishing inside, a captive in his own home, tied to a bed frame by his father. His fate sounded like a campfire tale, but it was essentially true. He and two schoolmates—Robert Baggett and Elliott Sawyer, the sheriff's son—had been taken before Judge Murdoch McCorvey Fountain in 1928 for breaking school windows with a slingshot and burglarizing a drugstore. Judge Fountain decided that such enterprising young men could benefit from a year at the state industrial school. Baggett and Sawyer's parents agreed, but Boleware proposed something else for his boy. He asked the judge to turn Son over to him, because he could guarantee that his lad would never trouble the community again. Something about the look in Boleware's eye persuaded Judge Fountain, and so Son went home with his father.[24]

After that, Son Boleware was rarely seen by anyone ever again. At first, friends from the high school would crawl on elbows and knees to his bedroom window to talk to him. Word got around that he would gladly do homework for the football players. In return for his help, they took him for rides in the darkness after midnight.

But years passed and all the young people Son had known in high school moved on, and he was forgotten. His shadowy figure appeared on the porch after dusk now and then. Some neighbors reported hearing a parched voice from the Boleware place cry "caw, caw!" and incidents of Peeping Toms were blamed on him. Once, Nelle saw him resting in the shade and didn't find him so strange. But, essentially, Son Boleware was erased from Monroeville forever.

"Mr. Boleware ruined his son's life, I guess because it was shaming him," said a friend of the Lee family. "The man was *mean*."[25] Or as Calpurnia, the Finches' housekeeper, says bitterly in *To Kill a Mockingbird* when the body of "Boo" Radley's father is taken away in a hearse, "There goes the meanest man

God ever blew breath into."[26] In 1952, Son died of tuberculosis. The marker placed at his grave in First Baptist Church cemetery reads, TO LIVE IN HEARTS WE LEAVE BEHIND IS NOT TO DIE.

———

Nelle and Truman had more than enough to write about on South Alabama Avenue, whether they chose to exaggerate their material or not. Soon, the Lees and the Faulks saw them lugging the Underwood No. 5 back and forth between houses. The tree house would have been the ideal spot to write, but the 20-pound typewriter was just too heavy to shove up there.

So it was that the two children began the journey that would change their lives in many ways, but would also separate them further from children their age. Now they were writers. Sometime later, a little girl came over to Truman's house to play games. But after an hour, she went home. She told her mother that Truman and Nelle spent so much time talking and arguing at the typewriter that they forgot all about her.[27]

———

Nelle and Truman's friendship was interrupted suddenly in the mid-1930s when Lillie Mae, belatedly exercising her partial custody rights, took Truman to New York City, where she was living with her second husband, Cuban-American businessman Joseph Capote. From then on, until he was about 18, Truman Capote, as he renamed himself, returned to Monroeville for summers only. His father, Arch Persons, saw him less and less.

Meanwhile, Nelle Lee grew into a strong-willed, independent young person. We get a glimpse of her in Truman's first novel, *Other Voices, Other Rooms* (1948). Nelle is the model for 12-year-old Idabel Tompkins—a forceful personality, quick with a dirty joke, haughty, and angry about the constraints of her gender.

When the main character in the novel, Joel, expresses embarrassment about undressing in front of Idabel, she retorts:

> "Son," she said, and spit between her fingers, "what you got in your britches is no news to me, and no concern of mine: hell, I've fooled around with nobody but boys since first grade. I never think like I'm a girl; you've got to remember that, or we can't never be friends." For all its bravado, she made this declaration with a special and compelling innocence; and when she knocked one fist against the other, as, frowning, she did now, and said: "I want so much to be a boy: I would be a sailor, I would . . ." the quality of her futility was touching.[28]

Chapter 3

First Hints of
To Kill a Mockingbird

Nelle entered Monroe County High School in September 1940, a year before the United States entered World War II. Generally she continued to ignore conventions that applied to most girls. Although she had a boyfriend or two, everyone in her high school class of 120 students knew she didn't make much of an effort to entice them. In a photograph taken her sophomore year, in spring 1942, she stands with her English class on the steps of the high school. Unlike nearly all the other girls, her hair doesn't look as if it's seen a curling iron recently, and her chin, held high, gives her unsmiling face a slightly defiant expression.

She had outgrown her overalls, but she was not about to allow any male, teenage or adult, to take advantage of her. One day, Truman's footloose father, Arch Persons, drove up the dirt lane to Jennings's house out in the country, eager to show off his new red Buick convertible. Everyone greeted him, including Nelle and Truman. Jennings said that Arch only nodded at his son, but he "immediately noticed Nelle, who by this time had grown into a tall teenager about as big as he was. Truman and I saw Arch's clawlike hand slip way down Nelle's back as he hugged her. Nelle stiffened, acted surprised, then backed away."

Arch let them each practice driving down to the mailbox at the end of the lane and back, until finally he took off with Nelle alone in the car. "A few minutes later Arch returned, minus Nelle and holding a handkerchief over his nose," Jennings said. It was bleeding.

Later Jennings asked Nelle what had happened. She shrugged. "I drove up to the mailbox and he got fresh. So I hit him in the schnozzle. Then I got out of the car and walked home."[1]

Classmates at Monroe County High School decided that Nelle was unusual: someone whom it wasn't all that easy to warm up to, but who was definitely a person to be reckoned with. "You took her as she was. She wasn't trying to impress anyone," said a classmate.[2]

Doing what was expected just struck her as illogical sometimes. One day, Nelle and her friends Anne Hines and Sara Anne McCall stopped to watch some boys their age choose teams for a pickup game of football on the courthouse lawn. Nelle insisted, over the boys' protests, that they put her on a team. One of the captains, A. B. Blass, Jr., gave in and put her on his side, figuring she'd quit after a play or two. The center hiked the ball, and A.B. handed it off to Nelle. As she took off, one of the opposing players ran around the end to intercept her. Instead of dodging, she straight-armed him and continued sprinting downfield toward the goal line.

A.B. put his hands on his hips disgustedly. "Nelle, we're playing touch!"

The sophomore class of Monroe County High School. Nelle (second row from the top, farthest right) adored her English teacher, Gladys Watson (top row, center). (Photographer unknown)

"Y'all can play that sissy game if you want to," she shouted over her shoulder, "but I'm playing tackle!"[3]

On the other hand, she was not against all normal behavior. She was polite and well-mannered to adults, using "sir" and "ma'am" when spoken to. And her parents expected her to attend college. She looked forward to it, in fact. It was the same for most of her upper-middle-class friends. Nelle's friend Sara already had chosen to attend Huntingdon College, a Methodist women's college in Montgomery. A.B., the touch football quarterback, could talk of nothing except applying to the school of his favorite college team, the University of Alabama.

So Nelle's college plans did not surprise her classmates. Nor would they have been surprised, really, to learn about her admiration for two adults who had begun to exert a powerful influence over her plans. Both were women with a go-it-alone attitude. The problem was that they had selected different career paths. This dilemma over which direction to take would eventually be one of the most critical decisions of Nelle's adult life: choosing writing or law.

The first of her two role models was her high school English teacher, Miss Gladys Watson. Like an apprentice learning the craft of writing, Nelle willingly submitted herself to Miss Watson's instruction. Tall, blond, and angular with hipbones that protruded under her warm-weather dresses, Miss Watson lived with her parents across the street from Nelle in a yellow two-story house with a deep, wide veranda that ran around three sides. Her father, "Doc" Watson, was a three-hundred-pound giant of a man. Miss Watson, outside of being one of the best teachers of two generations of students at Monroe County High School, was also a quilter and a gardener. Neighbors were accustomed to seeing her in her parents' yard pruning the lilacs, tending the potted succulents on the porch, and yanking out weeds in the grass, her fair face hidden beneath a big straw hat. She remained single until late in life, preferring to devote her time to reading and teaching.

Because the faculty of the high school was small, students had Miss Watson for three years—sophomore through senior English, which included a semester of British literature. Looking back, most of her students counted themselves lucky to have been given a triple dose of "Gladys," as a few called her behind her back.[4] "I adored her," said Sue Philipp, a friend of Nelle's. "She was very strict. She gave you two grades. One was for your grammar in a paper—and you got a whole letter taken off for any mistake and that included commas. So I would usually get a 'C' for grammar and an 'A' for writing."[5] English professors at state universities in Alabama were known to remark to some of their most proficient undergraduates, "You must have taken Miss Watson."

Her classes always began with students receiving a blue booklet of grammar rules, a sort of early Strunk and White *Elements of Style*, which Miss Watson had personally selected. It was going to be their bible, she told them; they should never lose it.[6] Grammatical writing also was the key to developing a clear *style* of writing. She had students read their compositions aloud so that everyone could hear how good writing had three Cs: clarity, coherence, and cadence. As she listened, she leaned forward, sucking on an earpiece of her pink tortoiseshell glasses and saying in an encouraging voice now and then, "That was good, very good."[7] In her heart, little did her students know, she would have given anything to be a writer herself.[8]

Sometimes, when her students had grown weary of gerunds and so on, and their writing hands ached, she would read them a story, poem, or scene from a play instead. She was a gifted reader of Chaucer in the original fifteenth-century English. As she recited *The Canterbury Tales*, the travelers in the tales lived again as they visited the taverns, shrines, and waysides of England of the Middle Ages.[9]

Nelle worshipped her. From the time Miss Watson came into her life, she became devoted to British literature. After school, she spent time in the library looking up in an encyclopedia the topics Miss Watson had mentioned. And there was also one well-thumbed copy of *Pride and Prejudice* in the library's collection that opened for Nelle the intimate world of Jane Austen.[10]

Whether Miss Watson perceived Nelle as a budding writer is hard to tell, especially since Monroe County High School had no school newspaper or yearbook to showcase the talents of stellar English students. But if being in print really mattered to Nelle, she easily could have been—in her father's newspaper, the *Monroe Journal*, of which he was part owner. Mr. Lee wouldn't have turned down a submission from his hopeful daughter. However, except for a poem titled "Springtime," which Nelle composed when she was 11, no byline of hers appeared in the *Journal*.[11] After Truman moved away, she wrote only in secret, though not in a journal. Her desk at home contained personal essays, short stories, and limericks. But she never dared share them with her parents or siblings. "Not even the family knew the content of these writings," Alice would later say, "as they were destroyed."[12]

———

Nelle's second role model was her sister Alice. Alice Finch Lee, the eldest of the Lee children, reminded many Monroeville residents of her father made over. In most families, a son was the heir apparent to a business, store, or farm. But Alice broke the mold. She seemed destined and determined to follow in her father's footsteps.

Alice and Nelle were as similar, Truman once cracked, "as a giraffe and a hippopotamus."[13] Alice was a petite, birdlike young woman who wore black glasses like her father. She was obedient in school, conservative, and the essence of tact. All through school she remained at the head of her class, and she graduated from Monroe County High School in 1928 at age 16. That fall, she enrolled in the Women's College of Alabama, a Methodist institution in Montgomery, enjoying the privilege of becoming the first member of her family to attend college. Her freshman year, 1928–29, was one of the happiest times of her life.[14]

Unfortunately, it was also her only year in college in Montgomery. The stock market crash in October upended her plans—at least that's what she told friends. The truth was, her father had other plans for her. For years he had pushed ahead without the support of a helpmate because of his wife's poor health. Now that Alice was entering adulthood—and was clearly a very capable young woman—he began to shift more and more of his professional duties to her. And she quickly rose to meet his requirements.

The year Alice left college, A. C. Lee purchased a partnership in the *Monroe Journal*. As a smart business move, he cut Alice in as the fourth of four partners, giving the Lees half interest. Alice was only 18, but her father had every faith in her. He put up the cash, completed the legal paperwork, and appointed her associate editor.

He needed her there while he went off adventuring in state politics. Three years earlier, in 1926, he had been elected Democratic representative to the state legislature. Politically, he was a centrist, a "states' righter" (meaning he was wary of federal power), and a fiscal conservative (meaning he was against big government). He was required to be in the state capital regularly.

In addition, A. C. Lee's business interests were expanding. Since 1923, he had been pivotal in helping the town council electrify all of Monroeville. As a result, in 1929—the year he and Alice became newspaper owners—Riviera Utilities Corporation moved its headquarters to Monroeville and appointed Lee as its corporation counsel for the entire state. If that weren't enough, he also accepted a post as director at the Monroe County Bank. Alice was the obvious choice to be his representative in Monroeville.

Alice had her work cut out for her on South Alabama Avenue, too. Her job was "keeping the home fires burning," as she later put it.[15] Her siblings, Louise, Edwin, and Nelle, were then 13, 9, and 3, respectively. The stress of raising them added to Mrs. Lee's mood swings. Black housekeepers could straighten up, do laundry, and make meals, but Mrs. Lee required attention, too. Alice had to take over.

She stepped into all these roles for the sake of helping her father, to whom she was devoted. If she were to entertain any thoughts of marriage, she would almost certainly require a larger pool of smart, eligible men than Monroeville could offer. But for the next seven years, from 1929 to 1936, she put her young life on hold while she worked side by side with her father at the *Journal* and helped him manage at home.

Meanwhile, A. C. Lee toiled away in the Alabama legislature on a career that was not exceptional: his convictions were too rock solid for politics. During his 12 years in the state capital, he was proudest of making good on a campaign promise to push through a budget bill that put county fiscal systems on a pay-as-you-go basis, thus reducing deficit spending. He also sponsored a bill that substantially raised the pension amount awarded to several thousand Confederate soldiers and their widows still living in Alabama in the 1930s.[16]

As the 1938 election approached, he decided he would not run again. Ten years shuttling back and forth to Montgomery were enough. His personal life offered greater rewards. After more than 20 years on the public scene, he was one of the most prominent figures in south Alabama. In his hometown, he was unquestionably a guiding spirit: a highly regarded attorney, newspaper publisher, bank director, civic leader, and church deacon. His children Louise and Edwin were then 19 and 15 and responsible young people; Nelle was in middle school. Also, there was the other side of the ledger to consider: he was coming up on 60 years of age, and feeling he should concentrate his energy. For a man with many responsibilities, some of them no longer necessary, it was time to take stock.

Alice moved away from Monroeville at age 26 in April 1937 to begin a delayed life of complete independence. She found work as a clerk in the newly created Social Security division of the Internal Revenue Service (IRS) in Birmingham. Given time, and her talent for running things, it's likely she would have moved up quickly, especially since Social Security, as a governmental agency, was destined to grow into a huge bureaucracy.

But then, suddenly, Mr. L. J. Bugg, of the law firm of Barnett, Bugg & Lee, died. With L. J. Bugg departed, a once-in-a-generation slot for an attorney opened up. A. C. Lee discussed with Alice the idea of returning to Monroeville, conditional on her completing law school, of course, as a new partner. She hesitated.

She asked him if folks in town would view her as Mr. Lee's "little girl," or as a person with an identity in her own right. He answered that by the time she completed law school, she would be older than 30. Who would think of her as someone's "little girl"? This mollified her. But she was also concerned that folks might not take a female lawyer seriously—there were fewer than two dozen or so in the entire state, and most practiced in Montgomery, Birmingham, or Mobile, where professional women were not unusual. To this, A. C. Lee had no direct answer. Instead, knowing Alice as he did, he appealed to her love of a challenge: "You won't know unless you try," he said.[17]

So in 1939 she enrolled in night classes in the Birmingham School of Law. It was a demanding regimen she set for herself: working full-time during the day and sitting through lectures at night. Nevertheless, attending school part-time, she completed her last semester at the end of four years. Then, in July 1943, during World War II, Alice and three "4Fs"—men who had failed the physical examination for active duty in the armed forces—presented themselves as candidates for the legal profession at the Whitley Hotel in Montgomery.[18]

The complete battery of examinations, 16 in all, lasted four days. On the fifth day, the phone in Alice's apartment rang early. She had passed. Her father was elated when he got the news.

Thus Alice assumed her place as a second-generation attorney in the law offices of Barnett, Bugg & Lee, eager to begin. As a country lawyer just starting out, she was prepared to accept practically any case that came through her door.

However, there was still the question of whether people would take her seriously—someone fit to give advice on weighty issues of law. On this score, she faced a real challenge. In the beginning, few clients brought her cases of any consequence, and her fellow attorneys in south Alabama treated her as a curiosity. She looked too delicate for contests in a courtroom; but more to the point, she was a woman in a small town. None of the leading civic organizations in Monroeville— the influential Kiwanis Club, for example—accepted women. Church and school committees were all that were open to her. Hence, she was shut out of the higher circles of power in Monroeville, and in the whole county, for that matter.

Then one day she received a call from a Mobile attorney with an exceptional reputation. He told Alice that he had a wrongful death suit in the docket for the next session of the circuit court in Monroeville. Would she assist him? She was flattered; of course she would.

As it turned out, what he really had in mind was using Alice as a legal assistant. During the trial, she sat quietly at the table watching the old pros in action. Presiding was circuit judge Francis W. Hare, a Monroeville native and a Lee family friend. With testimony taken, and both sides having made their arguments to the jury, the trial was clearly winding down. Alice had not said a word. Then Judge Hare made a statement to the jury.

"It is customary in cases like this for there to be two speeches on each side. However, we have with us the youngest member of the Bar. And if this young lady would like to address the jury, I will grant her that privilege." Alice rose, walked to the jury box of 12 men, and gave a memorable speech for her side. "Judge Hare had paved the way for my acceptance," she said later, "and I was treated as a member of the Bar and not as an aberration."[19]

——•——

Thus, as Nelle approached graduation from high school in 1944 and was faced with making a decision about college and a career, her sister Alice presented an example of a woman who had overcome challenges that would have discouraged anyone less determined. To someone of Nelle's spirit, who always enjoyed a good tussle, physical or verbal, her sister's quietly combative style and choice of law was an inspiration. As far as Nelle's love of literature and writing, and the example of Miss Watson, was concerned, perhaps she could find a way to write, too.

Since Alice had started off at the Women's College of Alabama, that's where Nelle decided to enroll. By now it had been renamed Huntingdon College, for the Countess of Huntingdon, a sponsor of the Wesleyan Movement (the foundation of the Methodist Church) in England. Wasting no time, Nelle signed up for summer classes in June.

A. C. Lee viewed this latest development with undisguised pleasure. Around town, he started telling a little joke. With Mr. Bugg taking his eternal rest, and Mr. Barnett running the Monroe County Bank, the firm of Barnett, Bugg & Lee might have to be changed one day to "Lee & Daughters, Attorneys"![20]

——•——

Actually, there couldn't have been a less appropriate school than Huntingdon College for a young woman like Nelle. Perhaps she was trying too hard to imitate her sister, or maybe she was also trying to please her mother by enrolling in a college that resembled the exclusive Alabama Girls' Industrial School. In any case, it was a poor match.

Huntingdon's 58-acre campus was located off East Fairview Avenue in one of Montgomery's loveliest neighborhoods, Old Cloverdale. The area still felt like the country in those days. Each house was large and quite Southern-looking, with wide aprons of lush green lawns. Sprays of mums, coneflowers, columbines, irises, and day lilies looked glorious in the sunlight. Beneath the heavy trees lay camellias, hostas, jasmine, and impatiens. Husbands parked their automobiles off-street, in garages at the end of private drives.

As the freshman girls arrived with their families through the front gate of Huntingdon College, they saw directly ahead the administration building, Flowers Hall. To the left and right, extending along a low, semicircular ridge, were all the other important buildings that new girls needed to become acquainted with: the library, the student center and its tea room, two dormitories, and the infirmary. These overlooked a natural amphitheater called the Green, which served as a park, playing field, and the site of an annual May festival, complete with a maypole and May Queen.

Huntingdon was traditional. Experienced educators taught such subjects as composition, the history of Western civilization, philosophy, and theology. By and large, the Huntingdon faculty was made up of graduates from selective northern institutions: Columbia, Cornell, Northwestern, and Syracuse. Many of the female instructors were unmarried, and some gallantly said that the students were their family.

The students' Christian education was priority at the start of every day. Chapel was at 8:00 A.M. Missing services was inexcusable, unless the offender made up the absence by attending church elsewhere.

Another important component of a Huntingdon girl's education was becoming adept at the social graces. Dinner was never a haphazard affair. The girls ate at tables of eight. At the head was a female instructor. As the food was passed, everyone was expected to take at least a small portion out of politeness. The proper piece of silverware had to match the course of the meal. Now and then the instructor would peek under the table to make sure none of the girls had their legs crossed—feet flat on the floor. Once a month, on a particular date, the girls were expected to come down to dinner in evening dress.

Off campus, Huntingdon girls were required to abide by a dress code that included hats, gloves, dresses, and high-heeled shoes. An appropriate outfit for a day in Montgomery consisted of a skirt, a cardigan worn backward, a string of pearls, a black Chesterfield coat, white gloves, and a white scarf worn in blustery weather. ("We must have looked like a bunch of penguins," one of the fashion-conscious students later said.)[21]

On weekends, young airmen from Maxwell Airfield, located just outside of Montgomery, made a beeline for the Huntingdon campus. The ones who could get their hands on a car whisked away girls to Hilda's on the Atlanta highway, a lively restaurant with dinner and dancing. There were organized dances, too. During 1944, Maxwell Airfield hosted 18 dances featuring popular big bands, including Glenn Miller's. Usually there were three airmen for every girl, and with those odds, the

Harper Lee (far right) poses with fellow students during her freshman year at Huntingdon College. She felt out of place at the school. (Photographer unknown)

young ladies could have a different date every weekend night, if they wished.

———

Into this whirl of social activity arrived Nelle on the Huntingdon campus as a full-time student in the autumn of 1944. Credits from two summer courses, added to the 12 semester hours she was awarded for high scores on four entrance exams in mathematics, social science, natural science, and English, resulted in her starting college as a second-semester freshman.[22]

She was assigned to a triple room in Massey Hall where the housemother was white-haired Mrs. Hammond, or "Mother

Hammond," a much-loved figure who enjoyed playing the role of nosy maiden aunt. She wore pince-nez—glasses without temple bars—which pressed the sides of her nose like Teddy Roosevelt's. When a young man arrived to pick up his date, Mrs. Hammond made a show of examining him up and down as though she had never seen such a specimen. It was rumored she could smell beer from 20 feet away.

As she settled into her triple room, Nelle was the same as other adolescents in relishing her newly found freedom. She no longer had to cope with problems at home stemming from her mother's illness; hardly anyone on campus had a preconceived notion about Nelle Harper Lee from Monroeville, except for a few high school classmates who had also enrolled there. (These included Nelle's friend Sara.) A life of independence, fun, books, and ideas—all the things afforded by higher education—awaited her at last. The first quarter she made the honor roll.

There were many fine instructors at Huntingdon, but Nelle's favorite was Irene Munro, whose course on international affairs had extra relevance because of the war. In a number of ways, Professor Munro was like Gladys Watson. She was tall and aristocratic, a graduate of Wesleyan and Columbia. She and her husband spent every summer at their place in Massachusetts because, she said, they liked the "intellectual energy" of New England. She peppered her lectures with thumbnail sketches of people who had spent their lives in the arts and letters. She impressed upon her students the need always to think critically and emphasized that an education was not a commodity that could be purchased. "If you lost your lecture notes, would you forget everything you're learning here?" she asked several times. "I certainly hope not."[23]

In class was a junior, Jeanne Foote, who struck up a friendship with Nelle when they agreed that Munro's class was their
favorite. Jeanne brought her readings for the class to Nelle's
floor in Massey Hall, and the two young women stayed up late
discussing them, camped out in the reception area so they
wouldn't disturb anyone. "Those conversations were very important to me," said Jeanne. "I don't think that there were
others at Huntingdon—whom I knew and had ready access
to—who had these same interests."[24]

It was true that Nelle was more sophisticated than most of
her classmates about politics and economics because her father
was a newspaper publisher and a state representative. And except for her six years in Birmingham, Alice had lived at home,
so the level of dinner table conversation at the Lees' was probably higher than in most small-town households in Alabama.
On the other hand, Nelle was not *really* sophisticated—at least
not in the eyes of most Huntingdon young women, and in ways
that mattered to them. Acceptability was measured by how
closely one followed rules of taste, manners, and politeness.
And by those standards, Nelle's behavior got on the nerves of
some of the girls in Massey Hall.

To begin with, her roommates objected to her swearing, a
trait of hers since childhood. Catherine Helms, who lived a few
doors down in Massey, remembered getting steamed every time
Nelle cursed. "We were taught that if you had to resort to ugly
words, you had a very weak vocabulary and needed further
English study. Actually we were not sure what a lot of bad
words meant. We were ladies in every sense . . . at least, most
of us were. So, a girl who used foul language was a misfit in

every sense of the word. Nobody wanted to be around her. I never heard any of my friends use four-letter words. No one in my family did."[25]

Another annoyance was Nelle's smoking—or, rather, the *way* she smoked. Smoking was equated with sophistication, and students were permitted to smoke cigarettes in their rooms. But a girl passing Nelle's room did a double take when she saw her puffing away on a pipe![26] The image couldn't have been more at odds with an environment devoted to enhancing girls' femininity.

And to many of the girls in Massey Hall, Nelle's appearance was the last straw. She did not wear an ounce of makeup, only brushed her hair instead of curling it, and evinced no interest in indulging in any kind of beauty regimen. By contrast, looking through the pages of Huntingdon's yearbook, her classmates were attuned to the latest hairstyles and fashions of the Swing Era.

Not even the approach of a social event could force Nelle to conform. She skipped monthly formal dinners rather than be forced to wear an evening dress. When Saturday night came and the girls left for a night of dancing, she found other ways to spend the evening. Or she just went home for the weekend. The campus newspaper, *The Huntress*, fails to mention her name except two or three times, despite pages and pages about student skits, engagement announcements, visits by students to friends' homes, class and club elections, and meetings of campus organizations.

By midyear, the verdict was all but in: Nelle was different, and not in a fun or delightful way, but in a manner that ignored convention, which could be interpreted as a kind of insult to everything these young ladies stood for.

"I didn't have anything in common with her because she was not like most of us," said Catherine. "She wasn't worried about how her hair looked or whether she had a date on Friday night like the rest of us were. I don't remember her sitting around and giggling and being silly and talking about what our weddings were going to be like—that's what teenage girls talked about. She was not a part of the 'girl group.' She never had what we would call in the South 'finishing touches.' "[27]

At the end of first semester, Nelle's roommates kicked her out.

Against the larger canvas of the campus, however, she made a different impression. Viewed from a distance, traits that set her apart from the normal Huntingdon "penguins" seemed intriguing. Walking across campus with her long stride, dressed in a simple navy cotton skirt, white blouse, and the brown leather bombardier's jacket her brother Edwin had given her (he was a flyer with the Eighth Army Air Corps), she cut a figure that blurred gender distinctions. "I noticed her physically," said Mary Benson Tomlinson, another freshman. "She had a presence. I remember her better than I do anyone else at Huntingdon, except my roommate and maybe one or two other people. Everything about her hinted at masculinity. I think the word 'handsome' would have suited her."[28]

Nelle's athleticism caught the attention of team captains. For volleyball games, she was first pick when choosing sides.

The solid *thunk!* of her spikes over the net resounded across the green. Her soccer kicks sent the other team running pell-mell after the ball.

She was not incapable of making friends, either, if given the chance. A chat with her after class revealed a bubbling sense of humor. "Every time I think about her, I always think about laughing, I always think about humor," said algebra classmate Martha Brown. Tina Rood, another classmate, agreed: "She really sort of became a recluse—even in school she did her thing—I just remember her as fun, and funny! I can still see her telling wonderful stories with a cigarette dangling from her lips."[29]

It took a while to get to know Nelle, but those who did realized something about her. She just wanted to be comfortable in her own skin. Her cussing was unconscious; the clothes she wore appealed to her because they were practical; she laughed when one of her teasing remarks drew a comeback delivered with equal zest. But she would not stop to seek others' approval. Her right to live as she pleased was not up for negotiation. It was nobody's business. "That was an era when you did the proper thing," said Catherine. "And your mother was horrified if you didn't. That was never part of Nelle's persona—she didn't care! It must have taken a colossal amount of courage to be different."[30]

Despite this, she was not unaware of other people's feelings. On February 12, 1945, half an hour before the girls were to come down in formal attire for a Valentine's Day dinner, a tornado tore through Montgomery, dragging a funnel for 13 miles that killed 26 people and destroyed 100 homes. The lights stayed off in Massey Hall until almost bedtime. By then, a girl in Nelle's dorm was too upset to sleep and kept looking out the window. For the next several days, fear of another tornado kept her awake.

"One afternoon," said the girl's roommate, Mary Nell Atherton, "Nelle came down to the room because she'd heard my roommate was so afraid she couldn't sleep. She told her, 'I'd be glad to stay up with you and keep you company, because I can't sleep, either.' Nelle was very concerned about people, but she was not one to mix and mingle that much."[31]

———

Although Nelle was sidelined socially at Huntingdon, she more than made up for it by contributing articles to *The Huntress*, the campus newspaper. In April, she was inducted with seven other girls into the campus chapter of the national literary society, Chi Delta Phi. Also that spring, the second-semester edition of the Huntingdon literary magazine, *The Prelude*, featured two sketches written by Nelle.

These short pieces of fiction, perhaps the first of Nelle's ever in print, stand out in the magazine, not only because the voice of a writer comes through, especially in the handling of Southern speech, but also because of the rather daring choice of subject matter: racial prejudice and justice, themes that would appear one day in *To Kill a Mockingbird*.

In "Nightmare," for instance, a Huntingdon girl is daydreaming in class. The droning voice of the teacher sends her into a reverie in which she sees herself as a "child crouched in the red dust peering through a broken board in a fence, her body stiff and shivering although it is August. She hears someone on the other side of the fence break into a low wail. Then comes the sound which she will hear in her dreams the rest of her life . . . Karrumph . . . Karangarang!" The child runs home and hides in her bed, but hears someone say as he passes under her window, "[D]idn't take him long . . . neck was pretty short . . . best hangin' I've seen in twenty years . . . now maybe they'll learn to behave themselves."[32]

To her Southern classmates raised in upper-middle-class circumstances, Nelle's decision to write about the hanging of a black man may have seemed in poor taste and outside the bounds of a college literary magazine. She may have submitted it as a bid for attention. Or she may have recognized that a subject with elements of conflict and social significance was worth writing about.

In her second story, "A Wink at Justice," also a clear forerunner of *To Kill a Mockingbird*, she takes a different tack. This time, in contrast to how bigotry permits injustice, she shows justice administered by a wise judge.

"The tiny courtroom reeked of tobacco smoke, cheap hair oil, and perspiration," the tale begins, anticipating a similar description from *To Kill a Mockingbird*: "The warm bitter sweet smell of clean Negro welcomed us as we entered the churchyard—Hearts of Love hair-dressing mingled with asafetida, snuff, Hoyt's Cologne, Brown's Mule, peppermint, and lilac talcum."[33] A swift overview of the courtroom borrows elements from the courtroom in her hometown of Monroeville she knew so well.

Then the judge enters, Judge Hanks—a dead ringer for A. C. Lee, right down to his mannerisms: "I saw a squat little man with his collar open at the neck and his tie askew. His vest was unbuttoned and his shirt was alarmingly wrinkled. He carried a pocketknife which he twirled constantly, sometimes thumping it up and catching it. Fine lines ran down from his nostrils to the corners of his mouth. I noticed that they deepened when he smiled. A pair of rimless glasses perched precariously on his short nose."

The case to be decided involves eight black men arrested for gambling. Judge Hanks comes down from the bench and orders them to turn their hands palms up. "He went down the line inspecting each outstretched hand. To three of the men he said, 'You c'n go. Git out of here!' To the other five he barked, 'Sixty days. Dismissed.'" After court is adjourned, the unnamed narrator approaches the judge and asks how he reached his decision.

"'Well, I looked at their hands. The ones who had corns on 'em I let go, because they work in the fields and probably have a pack of children to support. It was the ones with soft, smooth hands I was after. They're the ones who gamble professionally, and we don't need that sort of thing around here. Satisfied?'

"'Satisfied,' I said."[34]

As the end of her freshman year drew near, Nelle's reputation as a loner had jelled. The girls in Massey Hall had noticed that ever since changing rooms, she was often holed up, either in her room or at the library studying.

When word got around that she would be transferring to the University of Alabama at Tuscaloosa, northwest of Montgomery and only another couple of hours away from

Monroeville by car or train, one of her instructors, Dr. Gordon T. Chappell, professor of history and economics, expressed regret to his teaching assistant, Ann Richards. "He had mentioned several students that were doing outstanding work and she was one of them," she said. "He was disappointed that she wasn't coming back to Huntingdon because he thought she had a lot of promise. He was interested in the girls he thought would go far."[35]

During the final week of classes, in May, the girls in Massey Hall hugged each other and handed their yearbooks around, seeking farewell messages. In Catherine Cobb's book, Sara Anne McCall wrote, "Dear Cobb, It's been fun knowing you. You're one swell girl and I'll never forget you." Another student penned, "Dear Cobb, This year was really swell, and you helped make it so."

Florence Stikes handed her yearbook to Nelle. When she returned it, Nelle had written:

> Dearest Flo,
> Thanks for the memories
> of stinking sophomore lit
> of Mrs. Figh's shoes
> that you were so swell
> and now I'll leave you
> with love & all that hell!

"Typical Nelle," Florence said.[36]

Chapter 4

Rammer Jammer

"TA-*DUM*! TA-*DUM*! TA-DUMPITY-*DUM*!" SANG SEVERAL girls out the window of the Phi Mu house at the University of Alabama in Tuscaloosa. Their voices were loud enough so that the target of their ridicule could hear. "She had long flat shoes, long straight hair, a slight slump, probably because she carried a black, portable typewriter in one hand and a stack of books and papers in the other," said one of the choristers. "I never saw her with anyone and wonder if she were lonely."[1] The girl they were mocking was Nelle.

It seemed inconceivable that with World War II ended (on September 2, 1945) and the campus of 7,500 students full of veterans, any woman would not want to look her best. With a sea of men flooding the university, many co-eds hoped to get their "MRS degree" before graduation. The student newspaper, the *Crimson White*, added luster to their fantasies by featuring an undergraduate "Bama Belle" on the front page almost every week—lovely as a Hollywood starlet, sometimes with the distinction of being a gentleman's fiancée. A few were married already and pictured with their husbands in romantic settings, suggesting that a princess had at last found her prince.

But Nelle was apparently not interested in any of this, which affronted the young women in the 15 houses along Sorority Row. Her lack of makeup, her flyaway hair and dull brown outfits would have passed unnoticed had she been an "independent"—someone outside the elite panhellenic organization of sororities and fraternities. But she wasn't. Through an error of judgment on the part of the girls in the Chi Omega house, she had become one of them—a sorority sister.

Chi Omega was a house that "specialize[d] in blondes," proclaimed the university yearbook, "long, short, thin and broad," including Miss Alabama of 1946.[2] "Your [sorority] sisters were watching you," said one Chi O member. "They did not want our behavior to reflect on them."[3] And Nelle's certainly did. In the purely feminine waters of sorority life, she floated like a drop of motor oil. "I kind of wondered at the time what she saw in a sorority to join it," marveled another, looking back.[4]

The reason Nelle signed up for Rush Week at Alabama was a wish to be happier than she'd been at Huntingdon. Her sister Alice's year at Huntingdon had been immensely happy. But, then, Alice had joined clubs and organizations. Nelle had remained largely on the sidelines.

And there may have been another reason, too. A lifestyle where the accent was on femininity and grace was in step with her mother's values. Frances Lee, whose parents had invested time and money in making sure she was "turned out" properly, in the old-fashioned sense, would have approved of her youngest daughter going over to the debutante side. Maybe Nelle decided to give being her mother's daughter another try.

So with an optimistic heart, she put her name on the Panhellenic Association's list of young women scheduled to visit all the houses on Sorority Row during Rush Week in autumn 1945. As she and other rushees came through the door at Chi Omega, the members—all sporting fraternity pins—serenaded them lustily with fraternity songs. Nelle liked the humor. They invited her back. And a few days later, much to Nelle's surprise (and later theirs), the Chi Os—Nu Beta chapter, founded 1922—accepted her.

The Chi Omegas lived in a two-story brick house painted white, designed in the Federal style. On the right-hand side of the main stairway was a flat-roofed sunroom, sometimes used as extra sleeping quarters. Upstairs, the young women slept in bunk beds and got ready for the day by sharing showers and dressing rooms.

Once the girls came down in the morning, maids scurried upstairs to dust, sweep, and change the sheets. During mealtimes, the black butler served at table. Nelle usually skipped breakfast; she hated it because she hated eggs. And she let it be known that she hated swing music, too, which was then the most popular kind in America: she thought numbers by Benny Goodman, Count Basie, and Duke Ellington were frantic and obnoxious. She sang in the shower, but instead of catchy numbers such as "Let It Snow," her pretty alto voice carried songs by Gilbert and Sullivan, composers of nineteenth-century British musicals such as *The Mikado* and *H.M.S. Pinafore*.

A British tar is a soaring soul,

As free as a mountain bird,

His energetic fist should be ready to resist

A dictatorial word.

His nose should pant and his lip should curl,

His cheeks should flame and his brow should furl,

His bosom should heave and his heart should glow,

And his fist be ever ready for a knock-down blow.

Not a lot about her had changed since Huntingdon. She was still chain-smoking, and she preferred men's pajamas to nightgowns. "She was a little mannish-looking," recalled one sorority sister. "When girls had long hair and did things with it, her hair was short."[5] Another chose the word *matronly* to describe Nelle: "A little bit thick in the middle. Nothing very stylish." However, "she had beautiful large, dark brown eyes that were quite piercing."[6]

In the evenings, the girls chattered about their days and their boyfriends, but not Nelle. "She was just sort of a loner. She just sat there and looked. I don't remember any contact between her and anybody," said a sorority sister. At mealtimes, "she never entered into any conversations with the girls at the table, but was more of an observer. I always had the feeling that she found us very shallow, silly, and young in which case she was absolutely right."[7]

On Friday and Saturday nights, when the other Chi O girls were bustling around, trying to be ready in time for dates or dances, Nelle never had any plans. No one recalled seeing her with a boyfriend. Practically every weekend, she tromped through the living room, golf club bag slung over her shoulder, heading out for a few rounds. The way she dressed for the golf course, just jeans and a sweatshirt, raised a few eyebrows. "That wasn't the way we dressed," said a Chi O sister.[8] The pronouncement on Nelle's outerwear was that it was "very different."

"I'm ashamed to admit that we made fun of her," said Barbara Moore, a member of Phi Mu sorority. "Never around her, but behind her back. Today she would be called a campus nerd."[9]

———

After a year in the Chi Omega house, Nelle moved out. She would sometimes take her meals at the house and attended chapter meetings, but her sorority sisters thought she had her mind on other things. The reason was she had discovered a more suitable group of friends—commentators on campus life and its traditions and, most important, serious writers. She called them "the most casual colony" at the university, and they greeted her as one of their own. They were "the various editors, feature writers, proofreaders and kibitzers who sling together," as she put it, the University of Alabama campus publications.[10]

Nelle had found her way to the enormous Alabama Union almost as soon as she arrived on campus the fall of her sophomore year. On the third floor was the office of the student publications, a large room divided by a row of file cabinets acting as a line separating journalism from creative writing. On one side sat the staff of the *Crimson White* campus newspaper; on the other, the writers and editors for the *Rammer Jammer*, the campus humor magazine, named for the thunderous cheer shouted by Crimson Tide football fans: "Rammer jammer, rammer jammer, rammer jammer!"

Nelle introduced herself to one of the *Crimson White* editors, Bill Mayes, "a lanky, Klan-hating six-footer from somewhere in Mississippi."[11] She offered her services as a stringer—someone to cover the odd meeting or event now and then. But most of the news beats had already gone to journalism majors.

Not discouraged, she went around the wall of file cabinets to the *Rammer Jammer* side of the room. That staff consisted of novice satirists and humor writers, under pressure to produce a funny quarterly publication. Good submissions were sought after and prized. Nelle got her hand in right away by submitting a few pieces for the homecoming parody—a takeoff on *Esquire*, a fashion magazine for men. In the December issue, the masthead listed her name as a staff member. A *Crimson White* staffer recalled hearing Nelle's voice on the *Rammer Jammer* side of the file cabinets, and years later, when she read *To Kill a Mockingbird*, said, "I could just hear her talking in the book."[12]

During the following summer, Nelle stayed on campus, catching up on a few credits but also because she knew the *Crimson White* would need writers. She suggested an idea to Bill Mayes, who was taking over as summer newspaper editor: What if she wrote an at-large column, she asked, that commented on the passing scene—something to lighten up the editorial page? He agreed. For a non–journalism major, it was a coup.

She dubbed her column "Caustic Comment," an irregular feature that delivered doses of self-parody, exaggerated descriptions, and long-winded gags. John T. Hamner, a newspaperman in Alabama, was struck by the tone of "bright, brittle, sophomoric but sharp humor. . . . Her specialty was debunking, taking quick sharp jabs at the idols and mores of the time and place."[13] The column was at its strongest when Nelle took aim at silly advertisements on the radio, or the amount of red tape students had to endure. She didn't bother to conceal her fondness for cursing, either:

> There is a striking difference between University students now and those of five years ago in regard to their interests. Formerly, the minds of the Capstone [University of Alabama] undergrads were almost solely occupied with who belonged to what fraternity and the respective merits of Glenn Miller and Tommy Dorsey as bandleaders.
>
> The high moment in an undergrad's life was the interfraternity dances at the end of each year. He planned for months ahead just who he would escort to each dance, and how many invitations to pre-dance cocktail parties it would be socially acceptable to decline. He frantically rushed around trying to find the correct tie to wear with tails, and he considered himself a bright and shining social light if he wore clothes exactly like someone else's.
>
> Contrast the undergrad of 1946. He doesn't give a damn what kind of pants he wears to a formal, his major interests are not who's pinned to whom or how many quarts per capita his fraternity brothers consume each day. There is an awakening of interest in the lives of students in the things that really count.[14]

At times she used shock value to get readers' attention. Writing a book review, for instance, she interjected some tough talk about race relations, a subject usually avoided in polite company.

In her opinion, too many Southern writers treated racism romantically. For avoiding this pitfall, she praised the book under review, *Night Fire*, written by a popular instructor on campus, Edward Kimbrough. She relished Kimbrough's portrayal of a character named "Turkey Littlepage, who is reminiscent of all the county sheriffs in South Alabama and Mississippi. Mean, utterly stupid, and with violent prejudices, Turkey tramps through the pages of *Night Fire* as a living memorial to all the miserable incompetents the South elects as enforcers of the law."[15]

Such language was not often seen in print on campus. The University of Alabama in the 1940s, the "Country Club of the South," as it was nicknamed, was a "profoundly conservative community," remembered a history and political science major. "There were a few faculty members who expressed reservations about some of the prevailing political and social orthodoxies, but they received little student support and were generally regarded as harmless eccentrics. The one subject never discussed, in my experience, was race relations. The prevailing view was that there was no reason to upset the status quo, and most were willing to continue existing conditions indefinitely."[16]

But the *Crimson White* wasn't the best forum for Nelle's outspoken opinions, anyway. She "dressed differently, ate differently, talked differently than most. She thought differently, too," said John T. Hamner, "and those differences made her stand out."[17] So at the end of the summer of 1946, when Nelle was appointed editor in chief of the *Rammer Jammer*, it seemed at last that she could give her pen full throttle.

The humor magazine was wide open for creative writers with an offbeat slant on things. Taking over the top spot was going to be a heavy responsibility for her. That first semester as editor in chief, Nelle also started law school as a junior, which the University of Alabama allowed undergraduates to do.

Regardless, she proceeded with equal energy as both journalist and law student. Her quirkiness was a particularly good fit with the humor magazine's reputation. She is an "impressive figure as she strides down the corridor of New Hall at all hours attired in men's green striped pajamas," said the *Crimson White* in a front-page article.

> Quite frequently she passes out candy to unsuspecting freshmen; when she emerges from their rooms they have subscribed to the *Rammer Jammer*. . . . Her Utopia is a land with the culture of England and the government of Russia; her idea of heaven is a place where diligent law students and writers ascend after death and can stay up forever without Benzedrine [like caffeine]. . . . Wild about football, she played center on the fourth grade team in Monroeville, her hometown. Her favorite person is her sister "Bear." . . . Lawyer Lee will spend her future in Monroeville. As for literary aspirations she says, "I shall probably write a book some day. They all do."[18]

When the yearbook photographer visited the offices of the *Rammer Jammer*, Nelle hammed it up by posing as a harried editor glaring at her typewriter, a cigarette burning perilously low in one hand.

It was demanding, preparing for the law school classes in torts, real estate, and contract law, yet Nelle managed the *Rammer Jammer*'s staff of 16, too. "She was a lot of fun, she just made it go," said one of the self-described "lowly persons" on the staff.[19] Nelle contributed at least one piece to every issue, including *Now Is the Time for All Good Men*, a one-act play making fun of a proposed racist amendment to the Alabama State constitution.

Her so-called Boswell Amendment would have required prospective voters to interpret the U.S. Constitution to the satisfaction of the local registrar. At the start of the play, Nelle introduces a senator, the Hon. F. B. MacGillacuddy, who argues strenuously for the passage of the amendment, which is nothing more than a trick to keep blacks from the polls. Once it passes, however, Senator MacGillacuddy fails the test, too, and is denied the right to vote! He appears before the United States Supreme Court, pleading, "My civil liberties are being threatened. . . . Whatta you going to do about it, boys?"[20] As a piece of satire, it was more mature in style and content than most of what usually appeared in the magazine.

Even though Nelle enjoyed her stint at the helm of the *Rammer Jammer*, at the close of the 1946–47 school year, she severed her ties with it. One year as editor in chief was enough. Her law school classes were demanding, and she was forced to spend most evenings studying at the library until midnight. Trying to balance writing with law—a combination she thought possible—was proving to be next to impossible. Something had to give.

Classes ended in May, and Nelle went home by train. For once, she didn't stay on campus for the summer session. She was needed in Monroeville to help with a happy occasion: the marriage of her brother, Edwin, to Sara Anne McCall, her friend and classmate since childhood.

Edwin was seven years older than Sara and, according to friends, hadn't given her a second look when they were growing

up together. When he graduated from high school, she was still
in elementary school. Later she enrolled at Huntingdon College
the same year Nelle did, but Edwin was in the Army Air Corps
by then. In June 1944, he participated in the Normandy invasion, flew support for General Patton's Third Army in Europe,
and received the Purple Heart. In 1946, Captain Lee returned
to Alabama and reenrolled in Auburn University to complete
his degree in industrial engineering. There he met up with Sara,
who had transferred from Huntingdon. They hit it off immediately and fell in love. The wedding was set for Saturday,
June 28, 1947, in Monroeville.

Inside the church, garlands of Southern smilax and tall bas-
kets of Snow Queen gladioli decorated the aisle and altar. Sara
wore a dress with a high collar, full skirt, and long train that
was a modern adaptation of an 1860 wedding gown on display
in a museum in Richmond, Virginia. The reception was held
outside at the bride's home, an innovation that not many folks
in Monroeville were familiar with, but the lovely coolness
of the evening persuaded them it was a grand idea.

Everything would have been ideal for A. C. Lee as father of
the groom, except that Nelle had arrived home troubled about
the direction of her life.

The crux of the matter was that she wasn't enjoying law
school. She had enrolled, she said later, because "it was the line
of least resistance," meaning that she realized how strongly her
father wanted to welcome another lawyer into the family.[21] But
she was discovering that she hated studying law—and that was
the term she used, *hated*. A friend on the campus newspaper
never doubted that "she could have been a good lawyer. Her
mind was so quick, but she just wanted to write."[22]

If she framed her dilemma in similar terms to her father—that writing was winning out over law—he might have countered that she could take over the *Monroe Journal* from him and Alice. After all, he was almost 70. He was looking forward to having a little more time for playing golf and serving on various committees in ways that weren't too demanding. Just taking it easy. Weekly deadlines wouldn't permit that, and Alice's law practice was booming. So Nelle could do a real service by her family, the town, and the whole county if she took over the reins of the *Journal* after graduation. She didn't have to join Barnett, Bugg & Lee, either, if she didn't want to. But a law degree was always good insurance.

The rest of the summer must have been a bittersweet one in the Lee household. Edwin had made a fine marriage and let it be known that the couple would be settling down in Monroeville. Alice had decided to live at home permanently to help her parents, particularly her mother, whose health required regular visits to Vaughn Memorial Hospital in Selma, 75 miles away. Nelle, on the other hand, had thrown everybody for a loop. In August, she boarded the train at Evergreen and rode it north to Tuscaloosa, where she was determined to give law school one more try.

About 100 students were enrolled in law school for the 1947–48 school year, taught by 13 faculty members, all of whom were "on the younger side," remembered Nelle's classmate Daniel J. Meador, who would one day become an assistant attorney general in the U.S. Department of Justice. The number of women, however, he said, totaled less than a dozen. The whole group was small enough to fit "in the women's rest room at the same time."[23]

And they could usually be found in there, too, freshening

up between classes. Nelle milled around in front of the mirrors
with the others, but Mary Lee Stapp couldn't recall ever having
a conversation with her, "and she wouldn't have initiated it.
She never made a great effort to get to know anybody; she had
her mind on what she had her mind on."[24] Jane Williams
recalled Nelle from criminal law class, but "she would not have
been noticed except for the fact that she was in a large class of
males. She was habitually dressed in a baggy pullover, with a
skirt and loafers—her hair pulled behind her ears and no
makeup. To say that she was reclusive is an understatement.
She was very quiet, spoke to no one—except when the instructor called on her to respond. Even then, she did so with as few
words as possible."[25]

The women, although they were few in number, demonstrated a tenacity equal to their male counterparts. None who
attended during the years Nelle was enrolled flunked out.
Moreover, they would not be intimidated. A certain criminal
law professor, for example, tried to fluster female students by
pressing them on the indelicate facts of sex crimes. One day,
while he was questioning a student about the details of a rape
case, attempting to maneuver her into a graphic description,
she cut him off in midsentence: "Look," she said, "you know
about the male anatomy—why don't you just tell us?" The
class laughed and applauded.[26]

Meanwhile, Nelle continued to linger on the margins, dis-
engaged. "Most of the women who were there knew each
other, but most of us don't remember her," said a classmate.[27]
To drop out, though, would disappoint her father. Still, the
dread she felt at facing exams she might not pass for sheer lack
of interest threw a gloomy light on her future.

Unknown to her (though she would have been insulted if she knew), some of her classmates thought that Nelle and the law would not be a good match, either. One couldn't picture Nelle abiding by the formalities of courtroom protocol. "I think lawyers sort of have to conform, and she'd just as soon tell you to go to hell as to say something nice and turn around and walk away. . . . I just couldn't see her being interested in that sort of thing."[28]

By spring 1948, it was obvious to Mr. Lee that his youngest daughter wasn't showing anywhere near the same enthusiasm about practicing law that Alice had. So he agreed to provide an incentive—one that would acknowledge Nelle's love of literature. Perhaps, he reasoned, she should have an experience that showed what a well-paying career like practicing law could provide, including the means to travel and write on the side. On April 29, 1948, the *Monroe Journal* announced, "Miss Nelle Lee, University of Alabama law student and daughter of Mr. and Mrs. A. C. Lee of Monroeville, has been accepted as an exchange student at Oxford University in England during the coming summer. She will sail from New York on June 16."[29]

It would be a pilgrimage to the land of Nelle's favorite British authors: Jane Austen, Robert Louis Stevenson, Charles Lamb, Henry Fielding, Samuel Butler, and all the others, who until now had lived for her only between the covers of books. And perhaps it would break the spell of her unhappiness.

———

On the morning Nelle arrived at the New York docks preparing to board the *Marine Jumper,* a converted troopship from the war, there was a festive feeling in the air. Nearly 600 young people were hugging their parents, posing for snapshots, and waving as they climbed the steep gangway. Nelle found a spot in the passengers' quarters on one of the double bunks; in each room, there was one shower for 35 people—"just like you'd expect in the army," commented one of the students.[30]

Then the ship got under way, assisted by a tugboat or two to point the ship's bow toward the Atlantic. When New York had at last dipped below the horizon, coordinators from the exchange program assembled the students for a series of orientation programs. They provided lengthy sessions about the destination countries, their religions, social life, and economic problems after the war.

There was no curfew, so the main deck on starry nights was usually dotted with travelers lying on their backs, feeling the thrum of the 10,000-horsepower turbine underneath them as the ship rolled through the swells at 15 knots.

On Friday, June 25, passengers prepared for landing at Plymouth, England. After hastily eating breakfast, they boarded a ferry to the customs warehouse. Officials and porters loudly explained how to locate luggage.

Then a four-hour train ride brought the spires of Oxford within sight, by which time the students were so hungry they were bartering rolls and fruit saved from breakfast. As the train crossed the Isis River on the west side of the university, Nelle could see Christ Church's octagonal Tom Tower, whose seven-ton bell has rung 101 times every night since the late 1600s at 9:05 to mark curfew. The welcoming dinner that evening was held in a centuries-old hall amid stained glass, carved beam ceilings 50 feet overhead, and wood-paneled walls.

Although she was enrolled in the seminar on 20th-century literature, she was permitted, as all the students were, to attend any lecture she wanted to on philosophy, politics, and economics, or general topics. It's doubtful that the array of scholars then could be assembled for a six-week summer session today. The faculty of almost 70 lecturers included novelists, historians, music critics, and scientists. In addition to lectures that Nelle was required to attend on Virginia Woolf, T. S. Eliot, Russian poetry, and Jean-Paul Sartre, for example, there also were at least three other lectures to choose from every day on such topics as free will, truth, political theories and moral beliefs, communism, modern painting, and the history of Oxford University.[31] For a young woman like Nelle, raised in a rural and economically depressed part of the United States, it was a feast for the mind.

After that experience, she lasted only one more semester in law school. She knew she couldn't go on. "She fell in love with England," Alice said later.[32] She had walked streets known to writers she admired and imagined herself in their company. What she needed to do now was to write earnestly. Truman had done it. His first novel, *Other Voices, Other Rooms*, published that year, had established him. She couldn't hope to duplicate his success the first time out, but she had to make a start. Staying in law school was pointless, particularly when there was a strong possibility she might fail the exams because she just couldn't muster the will to study for them.

So at the end of the first semester, 1948, she withdrew from the University of Alabama without a degree—not even a bachelor's, since she had begun law school her junior year and didn't

Nelle found her niche at the University of Alabama writing for the campus newspaper and as editor of the Rammer Jammer, a humor magazine. She "hated" law school, however, and dropped out. (The Corolla Yearbook)

Truman Capote went to New York City during the mid-1940s and was famous by 1948. His example inspired Harper Lee to leave Alabama and become a writer in the literary center of the world. (Henry Cartier Bresson/Magnum Photos)

take the final exams. For a short while she lived at home and saved money. Then, having "got an itch to go to New York and write," as Alice said later, trying to put the best spin on the situation, 23-year-old Nelle Lee prepared to move out of the family home.[33]

Her send-off from Alabama was not festive, mainly because of her parents' doubts about her departure. Her mother imagined the direst scenarios befalling her daughter. Her father was crestfallen that his youngest child had burned her bridges by dropping out of law school a semester short of graduation.

After saying good-bye to the rest of the family, father and daughter drove down South Alabama Avenue, where Nelle had played tag, caught fireflies in jars, shot marbles, and stolen fruit from the neighbors' trees. They passed rickety picket fences, 100-year-old trees, and homes where people had been born, lived, and died without ever feeling the need to venture far.

Then Mr. Lee turned south out of the square and left Monroeville behind, the white dome of the courthouse receding in the rearview mirror. At Repton, he caught Route 84, going 24 miles east to Evergreen. The Louisville & Nashville Railroad steamed almost daily into Evergreen, tugging a line of Pullman cars. From there, his headstrong daughter could begin the 1,110-mile journey to New York City.

For the trip, Alice had insisted she wear white gloves. But when Nelle finally arrived at Penn Station the following day, she removed them, kicked off her high heels, and walked in her stocking feet. Scout had arrived in the big city.[34]

Chapter 5

"Willing
to Be Lucky"

IN 1949, THE YEAR NELLE ARRIVED IN NEW YORK CITY, author E. B. White wrote, "No one should come to New York to live unless he is willing to be lucky."[1]

As every newcomer knew, the giant city had riches worth having, but at the time of Nelle's arrival there was practically no place to live. The wartime housing shortage hadn't ended yet, and apartment dwellers weren't budging because rent controls ensured that they already had the best deals they could get. No Vacancy signs were everywhere.

Nevertheless, Nelle managed to find an apartment—although without hot water—at 1539 York Avenue between East 81st and 82nd Streets, in a pleasant neighborhood seven blocks east of Central Park, and a block and a half west of the East River, on the East Side of Manhattan. It was an old German-Czech-Romanian low-rise community of taverns, grocery stores, newsstands with papers in East European languages, delicatessens, coffeehouses, flower shops, drugstores, and German-language movie theaters. The city didn't supply enough garbage cans, so some protesting residents dumped their trash in the gutters.[2] On windy days, cyclones of news-papers, bread wrappers, and cigarette cellophane whirled through the air. In the heat, squashed fruit stank and the flies were as big as raisins.

Nelle needed a job, of course, and the first one she landed was in a bookstore.[3] At least she might meet writers there, she thought. But she discovered that unpacking books, shelving them, and ringing up sales was boring. Not the literary life she'd expected. The pay was low, too, and her father would not have been pleased to see her walloping parking meters to dis-lodge a quarter for a slice of pie and a cup of coffee.[4]

Things began looking up financially in 1950 when she took a position as a ticket agent at Eastern Airlines. Then she moved over to British Overseas Air Corporation (BOAC) because employees could fly to Britain at a discount, an adventure she liked to think about.

In the evenings she sat down at the wooden door she was using for a huge desk and wrote. At first, the din of the city was hard to shut out: taxis blowing their horns, trucks, fire engines, and radio shows squawking through open windows. On sultry nights, people sat outside smoking and talking until all hours. With time, however, she was able to ignore the noise and settle into writing reveries. She was making a start.

But breaking her ties with Monroeville was not easy. Her mother's health was poor and continued to decline. The burden of shuttling Mrs. Lee to doctors' appointments had fallen on Alice because Edwin and Louise were married with children. Mr. Lee was 70 and simply not up to it.

Using her vacation time from work, Nelle went home as often as she could. One winter evening in 1951, a classmate from Huntingdon College caught a glimpse of her in Selma, Alabama, walking along by herself, lost in thought. The woman pulled over and offered a ride. Nelle asked to be taken to the hospital a few blocks away; her mother was there. Since she was clearly preoccupied with worry, there was no talk of mutual friends and the good old days in college. The two rode the rest of the way in silence.[5]

Mrs. Lee never left the hospital, and on June 2, 1951, she died. Nelle was only 25, not an adult long enough to have resolved the biggest emotional mystery of her upbringing, which was why her mother had practically ignored her. It was true that her mother was beset by a "nervous disorder," as the family described it. But how far did that go in explaining the absence of normal attachments between parent and child?

It was one of those questions that death makes harder to answer.

———

No sooner had the family begun to recover from the long-expected passing of Mrs. Lee than they suffered a second blow that staggered them. Six weeks after the death of their mother, Edwin died at the age of 30. He had been recalled to duty for the Korean War and one hot day, following a vigorous game of softball at Maxwell Airfield near Montgomery, he sank into his bunk in the officers' quarters to rest. The next morning, July 12, he was found dead. The autopsy revealed a cerebral hemorrhage.

At the funeral in Monroeville, several hundred mourners dressed in black surrounded the grave on all sides, including three ministers representing the major Protestant denominations in town. A. C. Lee, bent under the weight of a double load of grief in such a short space of time, bore up as best he could. He never could have predicted such a turn of events in such a short space of time. Being a widower was a stage in life he had been anticipating. But his son! Edwin had been an outgoing, charismatic young man. A. C. Lee had hoped that someday he would rise to positions of leadership in the community like his father.

Standing by the graveside, Nelle must have wished she could give her father a gift—proof that he was, as she said later, "one of the most beloved men" in south Alabama.[6] Something that would extend his legacy, despite what fate had decided.

————

Nelle returned to New York and continued the routine of working at BOAC airlines during the day and writing at night. It was a rather lonely life at times because she hadn't made a lot of friends.

There was a party-loving bunch of ex-Alabamians living in New York, but they thought Nelle was rather boring. One of the chief revelers was Eugene Walter, a native of Mobile, who kept a stuffed monkey under a glass bell jar and who was finishing a novel, *The Untidy Pilgrim*. "All the Southerners in New York would get together about every ten days or two weeks . . . ," Eugene said. "There was a community, like a religious group except it wasn't a church. Southerners always, by secret gravity, find themselves together. . . . You always knew, if there was any kind of trouble, that was like cousins in town."[7]

Nelle put in an appearance at these gatherings from time to time, often accompanied by Truman, who had lived in the New York area since his mother's remarriage. But to most everyone else in the room she seemed to be an ordinary, shy young woman in worn-out jeans and a tomboy haircut, ill at ease among sophisticates. "Here was this dumpy girl from Monroeville," remarked Louise Simms, an Alabamian and wife of jazz saxophonist Zoot Simms. "We didn't think she was up to much. She said she was writing a book, and that was that."[8]

It was through Truman, however, that Nelle finally made two close friends. It happened in autumn of 1954, during rehearsals of the Broadway musical *House of Flowers* at the Alvin Theater on West 52nd Street. Nelle wouldn't normally have found herself in the wings of a theater examining the mysteries of light boards, scrim, cables, and pulleys, but Truman had brought her along. He had co-written the playscript and lyrics with Harold Arlen, the composer of "Over the Rainbow" for *The Wizard of Oz*. As Truman's tagalong friend for the day, Nelle got to listen to run-throughs of songs and dance numbers for the show.

Helping to freshen up some of the lyrics was another young arrival on the New York arts scene, Michael Martin Brown, originally from Mexia, Texas. Michael was almost exactly the same age as Nelle's late brother, Edwin. "He was brilliant and lively; his one defect of character was an inordinate love of puns," Nelle wrote later for *McCall's* magazine. "His audacity sometimes left his friends breathless—who in his circumstances would venture to buy a townhouse in Manhattan?"[9] With his wife, Joy, and two small sons, Michael lived in a late-1800s two-story town house on East 50th Street, dominated by his ebony grand piano. He enjoyed nothing better than dropping down on the piano bench and performing numbers from his cabaret act for the entertainment of his guests.

Since Nelle lived only a ten-minute subway ride north of the Browns, Michael invited her over to meet his wife.

Joy Brown turned out to be an "ethereal, utterly feminine creature," in Nelle's eyes.[10] She had trained with the School of American Ballet and danced with several companies, including the Ballet Russe de Monte Carlo and Les Ballets de Paris. The three new friends sang show tunes at Michael's piano, or gorged on one of Joy's latest chocolate concoctions in front of the fireplace. "Common interests as well as love drew me to them," Nelle wrote. "An endless flow of reading material circulated amongst us; we took pleasure in the same theater, films, music; we laughed at the same things, and we laughed at so much in those days."[11] Michael and Joy listened as she confided in them her hopes for becoming a writer, and they applauded the stories she read to them in an embarrassed voice.

———

December 1956 arrived, and Nelle was still working for BOAC. More than half a dozen years had slipped by since her arrival in New York, and not much had changed in her life. Usually around the holidays, she tried to schedule a vacation to Monroeville so she could spend Christmas with her family. A trip to the balmy South acted as a vaccination against the long, dark, slushy months of winter that descended on the Northeast.

This year her supervisor said that she could have off Christmas Eve and Day, but, otherwise, she would be needed at the ticket counter. Her disappointment brought on a sudden bout of homesickness and sad memories. "New York streets shine wet with the same gentle farmer's rain that soaks Alabama's winter fields. . . . I missed Christmas away from home, I thought. What I really missed was a memory, an old memory of people long since gone, of my grandparents' house bursting with cousins, smilax, and holly. I missed the sound of hunting boots, the sudden open-door gusts of chilly air that cut through the aroma of pine needles and oyster dressing. I missed my brother's night-before-Christmas mask of rectitude and my father's bumblebee bass humming 'Joy to the World.' "[12]

When Michael and Joy heard that Nelle would be alone on Christmas Eve, they invited her to stay the night and through breakfast, too. It was only right, they said.

Early Christmas morning, Nelle opened one eye to see a little boy in footie pajamas eagerly commanding her to rise and shine. Downstairs everyone had already gathered at the foot of the Christmas tree and was preparing to distribute presents. Michael had built a crackling fire in the fireplace. The Browns were in an especially happy mood because Michael had received a financial windfall from his musical comedy special, *He's for Me*, slated to be aired on NBC in July. Things couldn't have been better.

The adults never exchanged expensive gifts because Michael and Joy, knowing that Nelle couldn't afford them, had introduced a game about gift giving: the person who gave the least expensive, cleverest gift won. This Christmas, Nelle was pleased with herself because she'd found two gems: a postcard portrait of someone Michael admired and a used book of witty sayings for Joy. With pride, she handed out her gifts.

And then she waited . . . and she waited. Nothing came her way. The Browns, smiling to themselves, let her wait a little longer.

Finally, Joy said, "We haven't forgotten you. Look on the tree."

Poking out from the branches was a white envelope addressed "Nelle." Inside was a note: "Dear Nelle, You have one year off from your job to write whatever you please. Merry Christmas."

"What does this mean?" she asked.

"What it says." They told her to total up what it would cost for a year to stay home and write full-time. That sum was their gift.

Several seconds passed before she found her voice. "It's a fantastic gamble. It's such a great risk."

Michael smiled. "No, honey. It's not a risk. It's a sure thing."

She went to the window, "stunned by the day's miracle," she remembered later. "Christmas trees blurred softly across the street, and firelight made the children's shadows dance on the wall beside me. A full, fair chance for a new life. Not given me by an act of generosity, but by an act of love. *Our faith in you* was really all I had heard them say."[13]

A few weeks later, Nelle wrote rapturously to a friend,

Have you had time enough to think that over? The one stern string attached is that I will be subjected to a sort of 19th

Century regimen of discipline: they don't care whether anything I write makes a nickel. They want to lick me into some
kind of seriousness toward my talents, which of course will
destroy anything amiable in my character, but will set me on
the road to a career of sorts. . . . Aside from the et ceteras of
gratefulness and astonishment I feel about this proposition, I
have a horrible feeling that this *will* be the making of me. . . .[14]

She would have to carefully budget the Browns' gift of
money, but it was enough to pay rent, utilities, and groceries.
She quit her job at the airline and soon her schedule fell into
place: out of bed in the late morning, a dose of coffee, and then
to work—all day long until midnight sometimes. All she needed
was "paper, pen, and privacy."[15]

Under this "regimen of discipline," her output soared.

———

Six months later, she arrived at the offices of publisher J. B. Lippincott & Co. for an appointment to discuss her novel. With
the help of a husband-and-wife pair of agents, Annie Laurie
Williams and Maurice Crain, Nelle had submitted a manuscript for a novel she had titled *Atticus*, which later became *To
Kill a Mockingbird*.

The Lippincott editors who assembled to meet her were all
men except one: a late-middle-aged woman dressed in a business suit with her steel gray hair pulled tightly behind her. Her
name was Theresa von Hohoff, but she preferred the less stern-
sounding Tay Hohoff. She was short and rail-thin, with an aristocratic profile and a voice raspy from smoking cigarettes.[16]

Among Tay's principal delights were working with eager

young authors. But she also spent lots of time with her bookish husband, Arthur, and—this was a near obsession—adopted cats in need of homes. As she studied the "dark-haired, dark-eyed young woman [who] walked shyly into our office on Fifth Avenue," her instincts told her she would like her.[17]

To Nelle, the meeting was excruciating. The editors talked to her for a long time about *Atticus*, explaining that, on the one hand, her "characters stood on their own two feet, they were three-dimensional." On the other, the manuscript had structural problems: it was "more a series of anecdotes than a fully conceived novel." They made a number of suggestions about how to address their concerns. Turning her head back and forth to acknowledge the remarks from this roundtable dissection, Nelle obediently kept nodding and replying in her gentle Southern accent, "Yes sir, yes ma'am."[18] She assured them that she would try. Finally, they wished her luck on a revision and hoped to see her again.

Tay hadn't wanted to discourage her. Even though Nelle had never published anything, not even an essay or short story, her draft of a novel "was clearly not the work of an amateur," Tay decided.[19] In fact, it was hard to believe that Nelle was in her early 30s and had waited until now to approach a publisher. "[B]ut as I grew to know her better," Tay said later, "I came to believe the cause lay in an innate humility and a deep respect for the art of writing. To put it another way, what she wanted with all her being was to *write*—not merely to 'be a writer.'"[20]

At the end of the summer, Nelle resubmitted her manuscript to Tay, who wanted to work with her. "It was better. It wasn't *right*," Tay realized. "Obviously, a keen and witty and even wise mind had been at work; but was the mind that of a professional novelist? There were dangling threads of plot, there was a lack of unity—a beginning, a middle, an end that was inherent in the beginning."[21] Nevertheless, Tay was convinced that Nelle's willingness to accept criticism meant the book could be molded into shape. In October, Lippincott offered her a contract with an advance of a few thousand dollars so she could continue writing full-time. She was elated and offered to begin paying back the Browns their Christmas "loan," as she insisted on calling it. But Michael, more experienced about the ways of publishing, recommended that she wait.

———

As editor and author got down to the business of working together, Tay discovered that Nelle's speaking and writing voices were very similar—funny, subtle, and engaging, perfectly suited for the novel with a Southern setting she wanted to write. Tay encouraged Nelle to keep writing in that vein about Monroeville and its people. But as the Lippincott editors had tried to explain, a short story—even a series of short stories with the same setting and main character—is different from a novel. A short story usually hangs by one incident or revelation. A novel, however, needs an overarching story, deep and big enough to encompass everything else, especially the ongoing development over time of related characters and themes. The engine of this unifying story has to include continuing tension arising from a major conflict too, enough to keep the reader turning the novel's pages. What story could Nelle write about, Tay wanted to know, that could pull everything else together?

For many years now, ever since the publication of *To Kill a*

Mockingbird in 1960, many readers, teachers, and scholars have assumed that Nelle chose to tell in her novel a version of the infamous Scottsboro Boys trials in 1931–37. But that's wrong.

The Scottsboro "boys"—teenagers, none older than 19—were nine young black men accused of raping two white girls in boxcars on the Southern Railroad freight run from Chattanooga to Memphis, as the train crossed the Alabama border on March 25, 1931. The public was fascinated by the story because of its sheer ugliness. During the first trial, in Scottsboro, Alabama, their legal representation came from an alcoholic real estate attorney and his incompetent assistant. Newspapers boosted their circulations by blaring the sexual and racist angles of testimony with headlines such as "All Negroes Positively Identified by Girls and One White Boy Who Was Held Prisoner with Pistol and Knives While Nine Black Fiends Committed Revolting Crime." The jury found all of the accused guilty; the judge sentenced eight of the nine defendants to death, with the exception of a 12-year-old who was considered too young to die.

During a second trial, ordered by the United States Supreme Court, four of the accused were released after all charges against them were dropped. Eventually, all of the Scottsboro Boys were paroled, freed, or pardoned, except for one, who was tried and convicted of rape and given the death penalty four times. He escaped from prison in Alabama and fled to Detroit. After his arrest by the FBI in the 1950s, the governor of Michigan refused to extradite him to Alabama.

These events, most of which occurred when Nelle was about the age of her child-narrator Scout, would seem to be the historical foundation of *To Kill a Mockingbird*. The racial injustice

during the Scottsboro trials is on display; the white juries' fear
of black-white sexual relations is obvious; and the courage of
the two highly skilled attorneys who finally won the case for the
Scottsboro Boys can be grafted onto Atticus Finch.

The trouble is, the scope of those trials was too big, too
excessive for Nelle's purposes. In her novel she wanted "to leave
some record of the kind of life that existed in a very small
world," she later told an interviewer.[22] The courtroom scene of
Atticus defending Tom Robinson from a false charge of rape, for
example, compresses a history of racial injustice into one hot
afternoon. By comparison, the Scottsboro Boys case—a dragged-
out national scandal involving nine young men and two
women—was huge and too far removed from Nelle's experience.

Nelle later stated as much years after writing *To Kill a Mockingbird*. In a 1999 letter to Hazel Rowley, author of *Richard
Wright: The Life and Times*, Nelle said that she did not have so
sensational a case as the Scottsboro Boys in mind.[23] Most likely,
she used a crime that shocked the readers of the *Monroe Journal*
when she was a child and her father was editor/publisher of the
newspaper. A black man living near Monroeville was accused
of raping a white woman.

———

On Thursday, November 9, 1933, the *Monroe Journal* reported
that Naomi Lowery told authorities that a black laborer, Walter Lett, had raped her the previous Thursday near a brick factory south of Monroeville.[24]

Both Walter and Naomi were luckless types, floating on the
surface of the economic hard times. In his early 30s, Walter had

done less than ten years in the state prison farm in Tunnel Springs, Alabama, draining swamps and cutting roads through wooded areas. The length of his sentence suggests that he was convicted of drunkenness or fighting. Naomi, 25, had drifted into Monroe County with her husband, Ira, and son. They were too poor to afford even a radio.[25]

Regardless, Naomi was white, and her word mattered more than a black laborer's. Walter desperately protested that he didn't know his accuser and that he was working elsewhere during the time of the assault. It may have been that he and Naomi were lovers, or that she was involved with another black man. If a white woman became pregnant under those circumstances, it was not uncommon for her to claim rape or to accuse someone other than her lover.

For six months Lett awaited trial until the circuit court's spring term commenced in the Monroe County Courthouse.

He was arraigned on March 16, 1934, on a grand jury indictment on a capital crime of rape, which carried the death penalty. He pled "not guilty." Ten days later, circuit court judge F. W. Hare—who would later jump-start Alice Lee's career—and a jury of 12 white men heard Walter's testimony. The case took an unusually long time to be heard and decided. It was not until 9:00 P.M. that the jury returned to the courtroom with its guilty verdict and fixed "the punishment at death by electrocution."[26]

However, the verdict didn't sit well with some of the leading citizens of Monroeville and the county at large. Objections reached the statehouse in Montgomery, and on May 8, the Alabama Board of Pardons and Governor B. M. Miller granted a stay of execution. Governor Miller reset the date of execution for June 20. A second reprieve moved the date again, to July 20. The reason for the stays, Governor Miller told the *Montgomery Advertiser*, was that "many leading citizens of Monroe County" had written to him stating, as he expressed it: "I am of the opinion and conviction that there is much doubt as to the man being guilty."27

One of the petitioners may well have been Mr. Lee. He was the publisher and editor of the *Monroe Journal*, a director of the Monroe County Bank, an attorney, and an elected representative from Monroeville. If his name wasn't among the "many leading citizens of Monroe County" calling for clemency, Walter's cause might have suffered. In response, Governor Miller commuted Walter's sentence from death in the electric chair to life imprisonment.

But it was too late. Walter had been incarcerated on death row in Kilby Prison, near Montgomery. While Walter waited his turn to die three different times, he suffered a mental breakdown. The prison physician wrote to Governor Miller on July 20: "It is our opinion that he is a mental patient and that his place is not here."28 Governor Miller asked the state physician inspector to examine Walter personally. "It is my opinion that the above named prisoner," the inspector replied a few days later, "the man whose sentence you recently commuted, is insane."29

On July 30, Walter arrived at Searcy Hospital for the Insane, in Mt. Vernon, Alabama. He remained confined to the state mental hospital until he died of tuberculosis, in August 1937.

———

The potential of Walter Lett's trial to inspire sympathy, and its power to cast light on a racist judicial system in a small town, made it the better choice for Nelle's novel than the Scottsboro Boys trials. Moreover, she knew the details of it well, as do many older people who still live in Monroeville. And in her imagination, she could see the hero, the attorney in charge of a fictionalized version of Walter's defense, fitting inside the Monroe County Courthouse with ease. She had seen him there many times. It was her father, Mr. Lee.

In fact, Mr. Lee had defended two blacks accused of murder, in November 1919. He was just a 29-year-old attorney with four years' experience when he was appointed by the court to argue his first criminal case. He did his utmost, but lost, as he was destined to do, given the times.[30] Both his clients were hanged. He never took another criminal case.

But now, as a writer, Nelle could use this episode in her father's life to create a character—Atticus Finch, who could defend someone similar to Walter Lett, the character Tom Robinson. By using her father as the model for Atticus, his virtues as a humane, fair-minded man would be honored.

———

With the major elements for her novel in place, Nelle set to work on *To Kill a Mockingbird* in the winter of 1957. As any successful novelist must do, she needed to create a convincing landscape for her reader to enter. So the setting of *To Kill a Mockingbird* is Maycomb, Alabama, a town similar to Monroeville. The time is the Great Depression of the 1930s. Maycomb County is so poor that the energy of life itself seems to be on hold. "People moved slowly then," Nelle wrote. "They ambled across the square, shuffled in and out of the stores around it, took their time about everything. A day was twenty-four hours long but seemed longer. There was no hurry, for there was nowhere to go, nothing to buy and no money to buy it with, nothing to see outside the boundaries of Maycomb County."[31]

Nelle's time frame is a three-year period in Maycomb between the summer of 1932 and Halloween night 1935. Truman Capote later said the first two thirds of the book—the portion about Scout, Dill, and Jem (Nelle, Truman, and a combination of Nelle's brother, Edwin, and Truman's cousin Jennings, probably) trying to coax Boo Radley out of his house—"are quite literal and true."[32]

To populate the streets of Maycomb, Nelle thought back on the inhabitants of Monroeville in the early 1930s: officials, merchants, churchgoers, and even the local ne'er-do-wells. After the

Nelle Harper Lee in the late 1950s when she was writing To Kill a Mockingbird, but calling it Atticus. (Papers of Annie Laurie Williams, Columbia University)

novel was published, some folks believed they recognized themselves and neighbors. Truman made no bones about telling friends, "Most of the people in Nelle's book are drawn from life."[33]

An interesting twist about *To Kill a Mockingbird* is that there are two first-person narrative voices: the first is Jean Louise Finch, nicknamed "Scout." She talks, thinks, and acts like a six- to nine-year-old girl—albeit a very bright one—who perceives her world and the people in it as only an insatiably curious (and talkative) child could. The second narrator is Scout, too, now an adult looking back on events with the benefit of hindsight. Sometimes the voices will alternate. For example, the adult Scout will set the stage:

> When I was almost six and Jem was nearly ten, our summertime boundaries (within calling distance of Calpurnia) were Mrs. Henry Lafayette Dubose's house two doors to the north of us, and the Radley Place three doors to the south. We were never tempted to break them. The Radley Place was inhabited by an entity the mere description of whom was enough to make us behave for days on end; Mrs. Dubose was plain hell.
>
> That was the summer Dill came to us.[34]

Then six-year-old Scout describes the actual moment Dill appeared and drama replaces explanation. The narration provided by the adult Scout is like a voice-over in a film.

A few critics later found fault with this technique. Phoebe Adams in *The Atlantic* dismissed the story as "frankly and completely impossible, being told in the first person by a

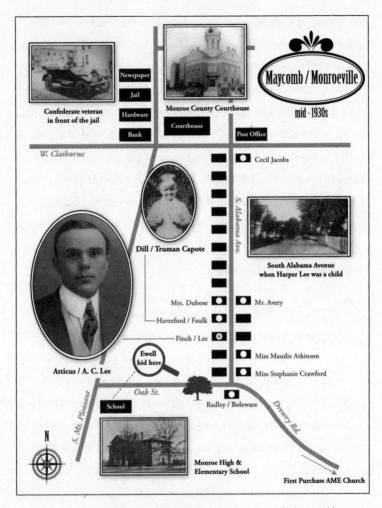

The setting of To Kill a Mockingbird *mirrors almost exactly the neighborhood where Harper Lee grew up. (Yoko Hirose, illustrator)*

six-year-old girl with the prose style of a well-educated adult."[35] Granville Hicks wrote in *The Saturday Review* that "Lee's problem has been to tell the story she wants to tell and yet to stay within the consciousness of a child, and she hasn't consistently solved it."[36] W. J. Stuckey, in *The Pulitzer Prize Novels: A Critical Look Backward*, attributed Nelle's "rhetorical trick" to a failure to solve "the technical problems raised by her story and whenever she gets into difficulties with one point of view, she switches to the other."[37]

It may be that Nelle had trouble deciding which point of view was better. She rewrote the novel three times: the original draft was in the third person; then she changed to the first person, and later rewrote the final draft, which blended the two narrators, who live both in the "present" of the novel and look back in time, too.[38]

In addition to her struggles with the novel's point of view, the effort of making progress on the story was so awful she almost gave up. A perfectionist, Nelle was more of a "rewriter" than a writer, she admitted later.[39] She "spent her days and nights in the most intense efforts to set down what she wanted to say in the way which would best say it to the reader," said Tay.[40] While working out of her apartment in New York, she lived on pennies, according to friends. No one "inquired too closely into what she ate," although now and then, another of Miss Watson's protégés living in New York invited Nelle over for a square meal and the chance to talk about how things were going on the book.[41] Then, for months at a time, Nelle returned to Monroeville to help care for her father, who had been in poor health since the deaths of his wife and son. During those visits, she went to the country club in Monroeville and found a room where she could write without interruption.

When it was necessary, Nelle and Tay met to discuss the book's progress. Tay remembered, "We talked it out, sometimes

for hours. And sometimes she came around to my way of thinking, sometimes I to hers, sometimes the discussion would open
up an entirely new line of thinking."[42] (She concurred with Nelle
about changing the title to *To Kill a Mockingbird*, from *Atticus*,
and about Nelle calling herself Harper Lee. Nelle never liked it
when people mispronounced her name "Nellie.")[43] Tay's main
concern was the structure of *To Kill a Mockingbird*. In her view,
Nelle needed "professional help in organizing her material and
developing a sound plot structure. After a couple of false starts,
the story-line, interplay of characters, and fall of emphasis grew
clearer, and with each revision—there were many minor changes
as the story grew in strength and in her own vision of it—the true
stature of the novel became evident."[44]

Even now, nearly 50 years after *To Kill a Mockingbird*
appeared, the rumor persists that Nelle Harper Lee didn't write
the novel herself. Truman Capote, so goes the whisper campaign, wrote large portions—or maybe all of it.

Tay Hohoff's son-in-law, Dr. Grady H. Nunn, said such a
deception wouldn't have occurred to Nelle.

I am satisfied that the relationship between Nelle and Tay
over those three years while *Mockingbird* was in the making
developed into a warmer and closer association than is usual
between author and editor. I believe that special association
came about at least in part because they worked, together,
over every word in the manuscript. Tay and Arthur became
Nelle's close friends, sort of family, and that friendship continued beyond the publication of the book. I doubt that the
special closeness could possibly have happened had there
been an alien ghostwriter, Capote, involved.[45]

Also, given Truman's inability to keep anybody's secrets, it's highly unlikely that he wouldn't have claimed right of authorship after the novel became famous. He did say, which Nelle never denied, that he read the manuscript and recommended some edits because it was too long in places.

Without question, the hard work of creating *To Kill a Mockingbird* fell squarely on Nelle, though "she always knew I was in her corner," said Tay, "even when I was most critical."[46]

Nevertheless, one cold night in New York City the effort of writing and rewriting almost got the better of Nelle. She was seated at her desk in her apartment on York Avenue, rereading a page in her typewriter over and over. Suddenly she gathered up everything she'd written, walked over to a window, and threw the entire draft outside into the snow. The manuscript of what would become one of the most popular novels of the 20th century landed in the slush. Pages of it blew down an alley. Then she called Tay and tearfully explained what she'd done. Tay told her to march outside immediately and retrieve the pages. They had worked too hard to give up now! Feeling exhausted, Nelle bundled up and went out into the darkness, "since I knew I could never be happy being anything but a writer . . . I kept at it because I knew it had to be my first novel, for better or for worse."[47]

———

Besides Tay, there were others in her corner, of course. Her second family in Manhattan gathered around her, giving her creative and emotional support. Michael and Joy Brown continued to depend on Nelle as an aunt to their children, and as Joy's best friend. Nelle's husband-and-wife agents, Annie Laurie Williams and Maurice Crain, invited her to their summer place, the Old Stone House in Connecticut, for long weekends. Nelle wrote them chatty letters from Monroeville during her visits home, catching them up on family news and local events.

Finally, in the spring of 1959, right before the final draft of the manuscript was ready for delivery to Lippincott, Nelle reached out to an inspirational figure in her dream of becoming a writer. She presented her novel to her former English teacher, Miss Gladys Watson, now Mrs. Watson-Burkett, and asked her to critique it.

At night, Mrs. Watson-Burkett would take it out of her sewing basket, jot notes in the margins, and discuss it with her husband.[48] One day after school, she asked a student, Cecil Ryland, to come up to her desk. According to Cecil, Mrs. Watson-Burkett said she had finished proofreading a novel by a former student and would he please run it over to her house. "And so, I gathered up the manuscript in an old stationery box, and took it and went knocking on her door. Nelle Harper Lee came to the door, and I said, 'Here's your book.' And she said 'Thank you.' Little did I realize that I held a little bit of history in my hands."[49]

———

That fall, Nelle was biding her time waiting for galleys of the book to arrive when Truman phoned in mid-November. An item in *The New York Times* had caught his attention, headlined "Wealthy Farmer, 3 of Family Slain." It read, in part:

> Holcomb, Kan., Nov. 15 (UPI)—A wealthy wheat farmer, his wife and their two young children were found

shot to death today in their home. They had been killed by shotgun blasts at close range after being bound and gagged.

The father, 48-year-old Herbert W. Clutter, was found in the basement with his son, Kenyon, 15. His wife Bonnie, 45, and a daughter, Nancy, 16, were in their beds.

There were no signs of a struggle, and nothing had been stolen. The telephone lines had been cut.

"This is apparently the case of a psychopathic killer," Sheriff Earl Robinson said.[50]

Harold Ross, editor of *The New Yorker* magazine, had assigned Truman to use the item as a springboard for writing about the impact of a quadruple murder on a small town. It was going to be a tough assignment. The Kansas story involved murder, and the killer or killers were still on the loose. Truman, slight, blond, bespectacled, was looking for someone to go with him.

His idea was to interview dozens of Holcomb residents and create a composite of the town's traumatized psyche. It sounded like an adventure that was poles apart from the drudgery of writing alone, and Nelle accepted instantly. "He said it would be a tremendously involved job and would take two people," she explained. "The crime intrigued him, and I'm intrigued with crime—and, boy, I wanted to go. It was deep calling to deep."[51]

Before they could go, however, they needed a contact in Kansas who was influential, someone who could open doors. Bennett Cerf, Truman's publisher at Random House, happened to know the president of Kansas State University, James McCain. Mr. McCain offered that if Truman spoke to the English faculty,

McCain would provide letters of introduction to key people in Garden City, Kansas, the nearest big town to Holcomb.

So, on the strength of this slim connection, Nelle and Truman prepared to travel by train to Kansas during the second week of December 1959.

They met at Grand Central Terminal, the most convenient location for both of them, and at about 5:30 P.M., walked to the gleaming 20th Century Limited, one of the finest passenger trains in the country at that time. They had a pair of roomettes reserved for the 800-mile run to Chicago, where they would catch the Santa Fe Super Chief going west. At 6:00 P.M. sharp, the train pulled out, heading north along the Hudson River and west to Buffalo. Sometime during the night it would turn southwest, along the southern shore of Lake Erie, and head straight for Chicago.

Then it was south to St. Louis, where they changed trains and continued on to Manhattan, Kansas, and Kansas State University. Truman spoke to the English faculty at the university, as promised. For the trip to Garden City, Nelle and Truman rented a Chevrolet and settled in for the almost 300-mile drive straight south.

Chapter 6

"See NL's Notes"

THEY ARRIVED AT TWILIGHT IN GARDEN CITY, A TOWN OF 11,000 on the high western Kansas wheat plain, as the sky was turning a deep icy green. The radio kept repeating the same bulletin at intervals: "Police authorities, continuing their investigation of the tragic Clutter slaying, have requested that anyone with pertinent information please contact the sheriff's office."[1] Driving down North Main Street, Truman and Nelle glanced expectantly left and right for the Warren Hotel. It was supposed to be the best and closest accommodation to the Clutter farm in Holcomb, a village of 270 residents, seven miles west on US-50.

They registered for adjoining rooms and then took the elevator upstairs to rest. The drive from Manhattan, Kansas, was monotonous, the last 100 miles of it through country so flat and featureless that a willow tree by a pond seemed interesting.

The next day, December 16, they walked a block to the Finney County Courthouse, the headquarters of the murder investigation. The person they needed to see was Kansas Bureau of Investigation detective Alvin Dewey, who had been appointed to coordinate the investigation by KBI chief Logan Sanford. Dewey was both a former Finney County sheriff and a former FBI agent. Chief Sanford had given him the additional responsibility of handling the press because he was not easily ruffled. In the field, a team of investigators was combing western Kansas for leads.

Nelle and Truman consulted a hand-painted directory on the first floor of the courthouse and took the stairs to the second. A secretary greeted them and escorted them to Dewey's office.

Alvin Dewey was "just plain handsome," Nelle decided on the spot, and made a point of saying so in her notes.[2] Dark-haired and dressed in a blue suit, he was seated at a mahogany desk positioned catty-corner in a cramped room. His mission as a lawman seemed defined by two prominent items in the room: a large map of the United States on the wall, and a thick criminal statute book on the desk. Dewey's brown eyes sized Nelle up—"a tall brunette, a good looker," he thought, indicating that Nelle had dressed well to help Truman make a favorable impression.[3]

Dewey invited them to sit down. His curiosity was piqued: he hadn't seen either of them among the reporters who had been hanging around during the past three weeks.

Truman, about five foot four and wearing a sheepskin coat, a long scarf that reached the floor, and moccasins—his version of western wear, apparently—acted as though he thought he was pretty important. Nelle took her cue from Truman and waited for him to begin a carefully rehearsed introduction. Dewey concealed a smile behind a drag on his Winston cigarette when he heard the sound of his visitor's babyish voice.

"Mr. Dewey, I am Truman Capote and this is my friend, Nelle Harper Lee. She's a writer, too." *The New Yorker* magazine, he explained, had assigned him to write an article about the Clutter case. Miss Lee was his assistant. Now they needed to get down to *business*. They were here to find out the facts about the murder, the family, and how the town was reacting.

Dewey listened noncommittally. They sounded like average reporters trying to get the inside scoop. "You're free to attend press conferences," he said. "I hold them about once a day."

"But I'm not a newspaperman," Truman insisted. "I need to talk to *you* in depth. . . . What I'm going to write will take months. What I am here for is to do a very special story on the family up to and including the murders."

Dewey indicated that he hadn't heard anything to make him change his original offer: they could attend press conferences with the rest of their kind.

"Look," Truman said, struggling to separate himself from newspapermen with daily deadlines, "it really doesn't make any difference to me if the case is ever solved or not."[4]

Dewey's face darkened, and Nelle sensed immediately that Truman had just torpedoed the mission. In fact, privately Dewey had been worrying for three weeks about the trail growing cold, and the dread of defeat was starting to gnaw at him.[5]

Anger suddenly got the better of him. "I'd like to see your press card, Mr. Cappuchi," he snapped.[6]

Truman let the mispronunciation pass, seeing that they were off on the wrong foot. "I don't have one," he said mildly.

The get-to-know-you meeting had turned into a showdown. Deciding it was best to leave, Nelle rose. Both men got to their feet. Dewey bid them a stiff good-bye and, after they had gone, returned to his work.

"From then on," Alvin Dewey said later, "he and his friend joined the news people at every conference. They were quiet, attentive, asked few questions, and, as far as I could tell, caused no commotion. I did hear they were hard at work, interviewing everyone, people said . . . in Holcomb, up and down Garden City's Main Street, in farm homes, in the coffee-drinking places, in the schools, everywhere. . . . Once Miss Lee broke the ice, I was told, Capote could get people to talking about the subject closest to their hearts, themselves."[7]

———

Nelle had accompanied Truman to Kansas as his salaried "assistant researchist"—a term he invented for her. Their assignment was to take a six-inch news item in the *New York Times* about the murder of the farm family in Holcomb, just a pinprick on the map, and find the humanity buried beneath the crime. They would have to find out everything about the family—Herb and Bonnie Clutter, and their children, teenagers Nancy and Kenyon—so the Clutters would be real. Truman wanted to accomplish all this without the benefit of taking notes or tape-recording during interviews. He was convinced that people were more guarded when they could see they were going on the record. He would just talk to people instead, conduct interviews as conversations.

Nelle's job was to listen and observe subtleties that Truman might be too busy to notice. Then they would return to the hotel and separately write down everything they could recall. Nelle's gift for creating character sketches turned out to complement Truman's ability to get people to open up. Many times over the next month, Truman's jottings would end with "See NL's notes," to remind himself to use her insights later.

If they drew a blank about a fact or a remark, they would prod each other's memories. In instances when key information was missing or unclear, they would have to go back and visit a person a second or a third time. "Together we would get it right," Nelle said.[8]

———

Ironically, one of the biggest obstacles to getting good interviews was Truman himself. From the beginning, he just didn't go over very well with people. "Nelle looked like normal folk, she was just a fantastic lady," said Harold Nye, one of the principal KBI detectives running down leads on the Clutter case, "but Truman was an absolute flake."[9] Mr. Nye, who at one point went five days and nights without sleep during the week after the murders, had no patience for snoopers from the big city.

Neither did postmistress Myrtle T. Clare. "Capote came walking around here real uppity and superior-like and acting so strange that I think people was scared of him. He was real foreign-like, and nobody would open their doors for him, afraid he'd knock them in the head."[10]

"I thought Capote was queero," said Gerald Van Vleet, Clutter's business partner. "He was nosy as hell and very, very

Perry Smith (right), one of the Clutter family murderers, receiving a mental fitness examination in March 1960 before his trial. (AP photo)

Left: Smith's partner Dick Hickock was talkative and friendly. "Never seen anyone so poised, relaxed, free & easy in the face of four 1st-degree murder charges," Nelle marveled in her notes. (AP photo)
Right: Alvin Dewey, a detective on the Clutter case, helped Nelle and Truman gain inside information about the investigation as it unfolded. (Corbis)

rude. He came out to my farm on a few occasions to talk to me, and I tried to avoid him."[11]

And there were key people who refused to be interviewed under any circumstances; they'd had their fill of reporters describing the gory details of a crime involving a respected family. For example, the first witnesses to find Nancy Clutter's body had been teenagers Nancy Ewalt and her friend Sue Kidwell, who had run screaming from the Clutters' house. When Nelle and Truman approached Nancy's father, Clarence, and asked for a moment of his time, he fixed them with his watery blue eyes, framed in a red, weather-beaten face, and said evenly three times to their questions, "I'm a busy man," and finally turned away.[12]

After several days of this, Truman began to believe that coming out to Kansas had been a mistake all around. "I cannot get any rapport with these people," he told Nelle. "I can't get a handle on them." Except for two high school English teachers who had read some of his work, no one knew him from the man in the moon. How many more times was he going to be called "Mr. Cappuchi" or "Ka-poat"?

"Hang on," Nelle said. "You *will* penetrate this place."[13]

A few days later they got their big break.

———

On Sunday, December 20, Nelle and Truman were waiting to be picked up in the lobby of the Warren Hotel by Herb Clutter's former estate attorney, Cliff Hope. Hope was on Dr. McCain's list of people to get to know, and Truman had been pestering him for several days. Finally, he had agreed to drive the pair out to the Clutter farm. The KBI had placed the farm off-limits, but Hope agreed to intercede with the family's executor, Kenneth Lyon, explaining that Nelle and Truman were friends of Dr. McCain's. Mr. Lyon acquiesced, but insisted on being present and drove the 200 miles from Wichita to meet them there.[14]

The farmhouse was at the end of a quarter-mile lane in Holcomb. Hope parked near the side. The yellow brick and white clapboard home with 14 rooms, 3 baths, and 2 wood fireplaces had been built in the late 1940s, at a time when many homes in the county went without running water. Surrounded by a lawn landscaped with pointed, jade green bushes, the big house had been the crown of Mr. Clutter's 4,000-acre farm. When Kenneth Lyon unlocked the front door, everyone started up the hedge-lined walk. The heat in the house was off, but the scent of lemon furniture polish hung in the chilly air.

In a way, Nelle and Truman had come full circle from their childhoods in Monroeville. They were figuratively once again on South Alabama Avenue where they had lived next door to each other and fantasized that a madman lived down the street in the tumbledown house owned by the Boleware family. They had spied on that house, speculated about the goings-on inside, and dared each other to sneak inside that lair. Nelle had used it, with some embellishments, as the home of Boo Radley in *To Kill a Mockingbird*. By contrast, this successful Kansas farmer's house, perched in a breezy, sunny spot, didn't have creaking hinges, broken shutters, and flickering shadows, or any of the lurid conventions associated with horror. But by exploring it, they were embarking once again on a hunt for something monstrous.

It took them about an hour to comb the house and the

outside. They went room by room, noting the furnishings, their color, the art on the walls, and even the books on the book-shelves. Nelle drew a detailed floor plan of the house to help jog Truman's memory when he was back in New York. In every respect, the house looked normal inside. The KBI had erased most of the gruesome evidence of the murders and returned the Clutter home to its almost museumlike emptiness and silence. Except for a bloodstain on the basement floor, there was no sign that four innocent people, two teenagers and their parents, had been murdered in the middle of the night. And for what? According to investigators, the only thing missing was a por-table radio.

Nelle and Truman thanked Mr. Hope and Mr. Lyon for mak-ing the house available to them. Van Vleet, Clutter's business partner, had arrived for the inspection, too, but he expressed his disapproval by sitting off by himself most of the time.

———

The day following the visit to the farm began the workweek lead-ing up to Christmas, on Friday, which would mean an enforced break from gathering interviews. The courthouse, library, and post office would be closed; even local law-enforcement authori-ties would be hard to reach. To celebrate Christmas Day, Nelle and Truman would probably have to fall back on a holiday din-ner special in the Warren Hotel coffee shop—turkey, gravy, instant potatoes, and canned cranberry sauce. It sounded bleak.

On Christmas Eve, Nelle spent part of the day assembling a description of the Clutters' last evening, based on several inter-views with Nancy's boyfriend, Bobby Rupp, who had stayed at their house watching television until 10:00 P.M. on November 14. Sometime after that, police estimated, the killers had arrived.

The phone rang in Nelle's room. It was Cliff Hope. "You and Truman going to be in town tomorrow?" he asked.

Nelle said they were.

"Any plans?"

None that she knew of.

"How about coming over for Christmas dinner?" He mentioned that he and his wife, Dolores, were having another couple over: Detective Alvin Dewey and his wife, Marie.

She and Truman accepted.[15]

———

The Hopes lived in a cream-colored, two-story house built in 1908 in Garden City—an old house by western standards—on Gillespie Place, a block-long street with a sign announcing PRIVATE DRIVE at either end.

Truman and Nelle arrived half an hour late because first he had to locate a gift bottle of J&B scotch, his favorite brand. During the introductions, Detective Al Dewey's wife, Marie, an attractive, dark-haired woman, explained her southern accent by saying she was Kansan by marriage but Deep South by birth and upbringing—New Orleans, in fact; to which Truman replied that he had been born in New Orleans and Nelle was from Alabama. "It was instant old home week," said Al Dewey.[17] Nelle, shaking hands, insisted everyone call her by her first name.

"Can I help in the kitchen?" she asked Dolores Hope.

"This way," Dolores replied happily. As the two women

took twice-baked potatoes from the oven and put condiments in bowls to go with roast duck, the main course, Dolores found herself liking Nelle right away. "After you talked to her for three minutes, you felt like you'd known her for years. She was 'just folks'—interested in others, kind, and humorous."[18]

Dolores announced that dinner was ready and the adults seated themselves in the dining room. The Hopes' four children—Christine, Nancy, Quentin, and Holly—sat at a miniature version of the grown-ups' table.

Looking around the scene, Truman realized it was a breakthrough in eliminating the town's suspicions about them, and he also knew Nelle deserved the thanks: "She was extremely helpful in the beginning when we weren't making much headway with the towns people, by making friends with the wives of the people I wanted to meet," he said later. "She is a gifted woman, courageous, and with a warmth that instantly kindles most people, however suspicious or dour."[19]

One of the Hopes' daughters, Holly, later author of *Garden City: Dreams in a Kansas Town*, said Christmas dinner that night brought together six people who became lifetime friends because they met on an intellectual level. "My experience in a small town is that there are always some people who have been involved in the arts and they like to keep up, but they might not have much opportunity. So when someone like Lee and Capote come through, it's a big deal. You just have to tap into it."[20]

By the end of the evening, Marie Dewey had invited Truman and Nelle to dinner at their house for red beans and rice—a real Southern dinner. It was music to their ears.

"Truman didn't fit in and nobody was talking to him," said

KBI detective Harold Nye, who by now was logging thousands of miles chasing down leads. "But Nelle got out there and laid some foundations with people. She worked her way around and finally got some contacts with the locals and was able to bring Truman in."[21]

They had penetrated Garden City, just as Nelle promised Truman they would.

———

Nelle and Truman arrived at the Deweys' the following Wednesday night about 6:30 P.M. Marie had planned quite a spread: a shrimp-and-avocado salad, red beans and rice cooked with bacon, corn bread, country-fried steak, and a bottle of a sweet white wine. Al introduced the guests to the rest of the family: Alvin III, 12; Paul, 9; and Courthouse Pete, a fat, one-eyed, 14-pound striped cat.

For about an hour, the adults sat in the living room getting better acquainted. About 8:00 P.M. dinner in the kitchen was ready. As everyone pulled up to the table, the phone rang again for the sixth or seventh time since Nelle and Truman had arrived. Marie said it rang at all hours ever since the murders—always a call for Al about some aspect of the case. He got up to answer while they waited to begin eating. From his office down the hall, they could hear him talking louder and louder. When he returned a few minutes later, his voice crackled with excitement.

"Well, if you can keep a secret, this is *it*: our agent out in Las Vegas said they just nabbed those two guys . . . Smith and Hickock."

Marie started to cry. "Oh, honey . . . honey, I can't believe it."[22]

For Nelle and Truman, the news squared with what they had figured out on their own. A rumor had been circulating among the reporters at the Finney County Courthouse about a prisoner, Floyd Wells, in Lansing State Penitentiary in Kansas, who read in the newspapers about the Clutter murders. Hoping to win a break from the prison authorities and claim the $1,000 reward offered by the *Hutchinson News*, Wells had told the warden about a former cellmate of his, Richard Hickock, who had planned to hook up with another guy, Perry Smith, and rob the Clutters. Hickock was convinced Clutter must have plenty of cash because Wells, a former farmhand on the Clutter place, had told him that there was a safe in the house.

All of this was supposed to be a secret, but now, in his euphoria, Al Dewey couldn't resist laying it all out for Nelle and Truman. The call he had just received was from Detective Nye. The Las Vegas Police had taken the two suspects into custody for a minor traffic violation. Mr. Nye had been doing "setups" in several states, alerting the police to be on the lookout for them. As soon as Nye, Dewey, and a third KBI detective, Clarence Duntz, could get to Las Vegas, they would begin interrogating the suspects, who had been leaving a tantalizing trail of bad checks all over the country.

"There's a lot of desert between here and Las Vegas," Dewey said, tapping a map with his finger. "On the way back, I don't care if we only make sixteen miles a day. We'll just drive around and around until we've made them talk. One or the other, whichever's the weaker, we'll kill him with kindness.

We've already got them separated . . . it shouldn't be long before we get them hating each other."

"Can I go with you?" Truman asked.

"Not this time, pardner."

Years later, Dewey insisted, "Capote got the official word on developments at the press conferences along with everyone else. Some people thought then, and probably still do, that he got next to me and got in on every move of the law. That was not so. He was on his own to get the material for his story or book. . . . That's the way things were when the good news finally came on December 30."[23]

Marie backed him up: "Alvin refused to talk about the case. We just visited, that's all. Our friendship developed in that way, but the investigation wasn't talked about."[24]

But Nelle's notes about everything that was said and done that night in the Deweys' home tell a different story.

———

Hundreds of Garden City and Holcomb residents prepared to brave the blustery weather, cold enough to snow, on Tuesday, January 5, the day scheduled for the arrival of the suspects from Las Vegas.

KBI chief Logan Sanford had said the suspects were due "late Tuesday afternoon," so Nelle and Truman showed up at the courthouse around 3:00 P.M. to wait for word from Sheriff Earl Robinson's office. The hallway was filled with bored newsmen smoking and waiting. Nelle found a Coors beer ashtray to crush out her cigarette butts, and settled in. A little after four, the radio dispatcher announced that the press conference would be delayed until 5:00 P.M. A highway patrol captain appeared, chomping on a cigar, and gave instructions to the press to keep the sidewalk clear. Nelle and Truman assumed a big crowd must be gathering, and went outside to see it.

An hour dragged by and it got dark. By 6:00 P.M. the crowd was four or five deep—teenagers, businessmen late for supper, and just curious townspeople. Newsmen stamped their freezing feet and blew on their hands. Nelle noticed Truman's ears were turning scarlet. Then suddenly someone shouted, "They're coming!"

At the curb, two dark mud-splashed sedans rolled to a halt. Al Dewey got out of the back seat of the first car. Quickly a handful of other men exited both cars, as if on cue. The figures strode quickly up the sidewalk toward the courthouse. It had grown so dark that the photographers' flashbulbs acted like strobe lights and caught them in midstep.

There were no jeers, no catcalls from the crowd. Everyone seemed strangely struck dumb. Detective Dewey had the arm of Perry Smith, who was a head shorter and wearing dungarees and a black leather jacket. Richard Hickock came next, also accompanied by a detective, but Nelle couldn't see him because a broad-backed policeman suddenly stepped in front of her. When the platoon of suspects and detectives sprinted up the courthouse steps, Nelle, Truman, and the reporters surged after them.

A press conference was held while the suspects were placed in their cells upstairs. Dewey sat behind a microphone to answer questions, but his remarks gave away nothing important—only that no one would be allowed to talk to the suspects. After half an hour, the television newsmen turned off their lights, and the press conference sputtered to an end.

Outside the courthouse, the crowd had dispersed, leaving

pop bottles and candy wrappers in the grass. Truman was dis-
gusted. He had expected the return of the killers to be dramatic.
Why had everyone just stood there gawking? And that press
conference! The whole thing, he complained to Nelle on the
walk back to the Warren Hotel, was "a debacle."[25]

———

Despite Al Dewey's announcement to the press that no one
would be allowed to interview the suspects or listen to their
tape-recorded confessions, all it took was a pair of $50 checks
made out separately to Perry Smith and Richard Hickock for
Nelle and Truman to talk to them on Monday, January 11,
with the suspects' lawyers present.

Al scooted a couple of extra chairs into his office. Perry
Smith came in first. Seeing that Nelle was standing, he waited
for her to be seated. He acted as solemn as a "small deacon in
his preciseness of posture," she wrote in her notes, "feet
together, back straight, hands together: could almost see a cel-
luloid collar and black narrow tie, so prim he was."[26] Truman
was ready with handwritten questions: "What is your feeling
about marriage?" "Have you ever wished to be married?"
"Would you say that you had a father complex—a combination of love and dislike and longing and fear?"[27]

Gently, Smith waved aside the questions after he heard the
first few. His attorney hadn't briefed him about this meeting.
"What's the purpose of your story?" he wanted to know. Nelle
was taken aback by his superior tone. Its purpose, they assured
him, was to give him a chance to tell his side of the story. Nelle
smiled at Smith several times, but his large dark eyes kept flicking

away from hers.[28] He clearly felt "cornered and suspicious," Truman realized. To everything they asked over the next 20 minutes, Smith countered with "I decline," "I do not care to," or "I will think it over." Some kind of cat-and-mouse game was under way. After he returned to his cell, Nelle commented in her notes, "Rough going."[29]

Richard Hickock, on the other hand, breezed in, ready for a good bull session. He plunked down in a chair before Nelle was seated. "Never seen anyone so poised, relaxed, free & easy in the face of four 1st-degree murder charges," Nelle marveled. "Can't decide whether H. thinks he's gonna get away with it; or has not realized the depth and futility of the trouble he's in. Speaks of the future as if he'll walk out tomorrow."[30]

She and Truman expressed admiration for Hickock's tattoos, which worked like a charm in unlocking his friendliness. Soon he was talking about his favorite reading matter (motors or engineering; his vision of the good life (well-done steaks, mixed drinks, dance music, and Camel cigarettes—he bummed five smokes from Nelle's pack); how often he liked to eat (three times a day, but in jail it was only two); how he'd like to get a good job in an auto shop and pay off the bad checks he'd written and live in the country. It was practically more than Nelle and Truman could absorb. Truman said Hickock was "like someone you meet on a train, immensely garrulous, who starts up a conversation and is only too obliged to tell you *everything*."[31] Nelle tried to get questions in edgewise, to which Hickock would reply, "Yes, ma'am," and then commence spinning another yarn.

He would have extended his stay, except that Al had

something he wanted to share with Nelle and Truman, so Hickock was taken back to his cell.

———

After Hickock had gone, Dewey reassured Nelle and Truman, telling them not to worry if Smith wanted to play it cagey. Reaching into the Clutter case file in his office, he produced for them the pièce de résistance: the transcripts of Smith's interrogations. Like dialogue from a play, the pages of transcribed conversation between Smith and the two KBI detectives, Dewey and Duntz, contained everything said in the 9'-x-10' interrogation room during the three and a half hours that Smith was questioned in Las Vegas. The transcript couldn't leave the courthouse, and was too much for Nelle to copy, so she targeted key passages. As she worked, Dewey added visual descriptions that weren't evident on the tape. Thus:

Al: Perry, you have been lying to us, you haven't been telling the truth. We know where you were on that weekend—you were out at Holcomb, Kansas, seven miles west of Garden City, murdering the Clutter family.

(Perry white; swallowed a couple of times. Long pause.)

Perry: I don't know anybody named Clutter, I don't know where Garden City or Holcomb is—

Al: You'd better get straightened out on this deal and tell us the truth—

Perry: I don't know what you're talking about . . . I don't know what you're talking about.

(Al & Duntz rise to go.)

Al: We're talking to you sometime tomorrow. You'd better think this over tonight. Do you know what today is? Nancy Clutter's birthday. She would have been seventeen.[32]

When Nelle had finished copying as much as she could, Dewey let her and Truman see another piece of evidence: Nancy Clutter's diary containing three years' worth of entries. Since the age of 14, Nancy had recorded, in three or four sentences every night, the day's events and her thoughts about family, friends, pets, and, later, her teenage love affair with Bobby Rupp. Different colored ink identified the years. Nelle and Truman riffled through the pages. The final entry was made approximately an hour before her death. Nelle copied it down.[33]

———

Loaded with notes from interviews, transcribed interrogations, newspaper clippings, some photos Truman had snapped, sketches of the Clutter farmhouse, and anything Dewey had given them copies of, Nelle and Truman boarded the luxury Santa Fe Super Chief on January 16 in Garden City. It was snowing hard, and they settled in for the 40-hour ride to Dearborn Station, in Chicago. Over the course of approximately one month, they had gathered enough for a solid magazine article for *The New Yorker*. They would have to return for the trial in March. If the suspects were sentenced to death, should their execution be part of the story? It was a grisly thought. Before his ideas escaped him, Truman wrote some notes on a Santa Fe cocktail napkin.

Nelle, of course, had plenty of other things to think about. As soon as she returned to New York, she would have to go over the galleys of *To Kill a Mockingbird*—a painstaking but nevertheless thrilling task for a first-time novelist.

As she watched Truman in the seat opposite hers, musing out the window of the train about *The New Yorker* article, it probably seemed incredible that her novel would be in bookstores in a few months. Then she would have the right to call herself a writer, too, though not in his league by any means. All she hoped for was a "quick and merciful death at the hands of reviewers."[34]

The Super Chief was delayed for six hours along the route, and when they arrived in Chicago, they had already missed their New York Central connection. They stayed in the city overnight and departed again the next day, arriving in New York on Wednesday, January 20.

"Returned yesterday—after nearly 2 months in Kansas: an extraordinary experience, in many ways the most interesting thing that's ever happened to me," Truman wrote to his friend, the photographer Cecil Beaton. "But I will let you read about it—it may amount to a small book."[35]

That small book, *In Cold Blood*, would become one of the most highly regarded works of nonfiction ever published.

———

Two months later, Nelle and Truman were back in Kansas for the trial, scheduled to begin the third week of March. By coincidence, the Clutters' farm was going up for auction the same week.

They left behind a late snowy season in New York. A wet,

warm spring had come to western Kansas. Nelle and Truman drove out to the Clutter farm on Sunday, March 21, to witness the sale. Bumper-to-bumper traffic met them at the entrance to the lane up to the farmhouse. The sunny weather in the low 70s had brought out more than 4,000 people for the largest farm auction in western Kansas history. There were cars and trucks from Colorado, Nebraska, and Oklahoma, and practically every county in Kansas west of Newton and Wichita. Auctioneer John Collins, his white shirt shining in the sun, sold everything of value to a swarm of men in coats and Stetsons—tools, tractors, and farm implements.

On Tuesday, jury selection began. For the first time since the courthouse was erected in 1929, the varnished church-type pews were pushed to the sides and rear to leave room at the front for a special press table and 13 chairs. The newsmen sitting there, pleased to see Nelle back, had taken to calling her "Little Nelle."[36]

Just before ten o'clock, district judge Roland Tate entered. Overhead, the telltale metallic clunk of the jail door announced that the defendants were coming down.

The effects of sitting in jail for two months told on them. "Perry Smith is much heavier," Nelle noted; Richard Hickock, "fatter, greener, and more gruesome."[37] Outwardly, they seemed bored, covering perhaps for being stared at by the 44 prospective jurors who had assembled in the courtroom to be sworn in and questioned. District court clerk Mae Purdy called the prospective jurors' names in a droning voice. Only four were women.

By day's end, the jury was composed entirely of men, including the reserve of alternates. Half were farmers. Smith, an

amateur artist, had passed the time sketching on a legal pad.
Hickock chomped relentlessly on a wad of gum, his chin resting
on his hand now and then. The two men had implicated each
other in their confessions, but there seemed to be no break in
their relationship. Nelle saw Hickock glance at Smith just once,
"the briefest exchange of glances, and the old eye rolled coldly.
This was when the lawyers huddled the last time and made
their preemptory challenges on papers. Smith and Hickock
were left alone at the table. Perry looked at him—gave Hickock
one of his melting glances—really melting in its intensity—
Hickcock felt eyes upon him, looked around and smiled the
shadow of a smile."[38]

The turnout for the actual trial exceeded the courtroom's
capacity of 160 persons. At the press table, Associated Press
reporter Elon Torrence noticed that Truman, dressed in a blue
sports jacket, khaki trousers, white shirt, and a bow tie, spent
most of his time listening, while Nelle, bringing to bear her law
school training, "took notes and did most of the work during
the trial."[39]

There were no surprises. "How cheap!" exclaimed special
prosecutor Logan Green in his closing argument to the jury.
"The loot was only about $80, or $20 a life." Harrison Smith
and Arthur Fleming, attorneys for the accused, did not contest
the state's evidence but pleaded for life imprisonment. Harrison
Smith argued capital punishment is "a miserable failure." The
jury deliberated less than two hours.

On Tuesday, March 29, Judge Roland Tate sentenced both
men to hang. "When the Judge was telling the jury what a good
job they had done," Hickock told *Male* magazine,

I thought that these pompous old ginks were the lousiest looking specimens of manhood I had ever seen; old cronies that acted like they were God or somebody. Right then I wished every one of them had been at the Clutter house that night and that included the Judge. I would have found out how much God they had in them! If they had been there and had any God in them I would have let it run out on the floor. I thought, boy, I'd like to do it right here. Now there was something that would have really stirred them up!

When the jury filed out of the courtroom not one of them would look at me. I looked each one in the face and I kept thinking, Look at me, look at me, look at me!

But none of them would.[40]

This jury was no different from others in not looking at the defendants, Nelle wrote in her notes. "Why they never look at people they've sentenced to death, I'll never know, but they don't."[41]

Back in his cell, Smith slipped a note with his signature between two bricks in the wall: "To the gallows . . . May 13, 1960."[42]

Chapter 7

Mockingbird
Takes Off

In spring 1960, Nelle presented Truman with 150 pages of typed notes organized by topic, including the Landscape, the Crime, Other Members of the Clutter Family, and so on. Truman, feeling expansive as he rested in Spain after several months of working, was in the mood to make one of his gossipy pronouncements, for it was immensely satisfying to him that his student—which is how he regarded Nelle—had written a publishable novel in which he was an important character. He loved the idea. To his society friends, film producer David O. Selznick and his wife, Jennifer Jones, Truman wrote, "On July 11th [1960], Lippincott is publishing a delightful book: TO KILL A MOCKINGBIRD by Harper Lee. Get it. It's going to be a great success. In it, I am the character called 'Dill'—the author being a childhood friend."[1]

Truman, who liked to say he was "as big as a shotgun and just as noisy," was eager to broadcast that he was a character in a new novel, but his prediction that *To Kill a Mockingbird* would be popular was hardly a guess. During March and April, well before the book reached bookstores, responses from early readers had outstripped all Nelle's expectations. "I sort of hoped that maybe someone would like it enough to give me encouragement. Public encouragement. I hoped for a little."[2] So far, early signs promised far more than that: the Literary Guild had chosen *To Kill a Mockingbird* as one of its selections, and Reader's Digest for one of its Condensed Books.

In Monroeville, the news of a local girl making good led to an exuberant item in the *Monroe Journal*: "Everybody, but everybody, is looking forward to publication . . . of Nell [*sic*] Harper Lee's book, *To Kill a Mockingbird*. . . . It's wonderful. The characters are so well defined, it's crammed and jammed with chuckles, and then there are some scenes that will really choke you up."[3] Ernestine's Gift Shop, on the town square, scored a coup when the owner announced that Nelle would be holding a book-signing there just as soon as she was back in town.

Within a few weeks after the release of *To Kill a Mockingbird*, in July 1960, the novel hit both the *New York Times* and the *Chicago Tribune* lists of top 10 bestsellers. Reviewers for major publications found themselves enchanted by it.

"[I]t is pleasing to recommend a book that shows what a novelist can do with familiar situations," wrote Herbert Mitgang in the *New York Times*. "Here is a storyteller justifying the novel as a form that transcends time and place." Frank Lyell, in another *New York Times* piece, breathed a sigh of relief that "Maycomb has its share of eccentrics and evil-doers, but Miss Lee has not tried to satisfy the current lust for morbid, grotesque tales of Southern depravity." The *New York World*

Telegram predicted "a bright future beckoning" the author, and the *Tennessee Commercial Appeal* announced the addition of "another new writer to the growing galaxy of Southern novelists." The *Washington Post* began its review by praising the novel's power to carry a moral theme: "A hundred pounds of sermons on tolerance, or an equal measure of invective deploring the lack of it, will weigh far less in the scale of enlightenment than a mere 18 ounces of new fiction bearing the title *To Kill a Mockingbird*."[4]

Such praise brought Nelle unbroken, dizzying joy. Positive reviews meant that she had talent; she had been right to leave Alabama 10 years earlier and go to New York with the dreamy notion of becoming an author; right to seek out the publishing world; right to quit a low-paying job so she could write full time. And she had proved that she could withstand the rigors of first drafts, criticism, and rewriting without becoming discouraged.

What was happening was that the book had not been dealt a "quick and merciful death," as Nelle had imagined. In fact, it seemed to have tapped into the important concerns of the era—the growing national interest in civil rights for blacks, the appeal of a life set in simpler times, and the need on the part of Americans to see themselves as justice-loving in the face of Soviet-style communism. *To Kill a Mockingbird* struck a chord with readers.

But the novel's blastoff in the realm of bestsellerdom was not solely the result of penning the right book at the right time. There was another novel published about the South that summer: Leon Odell Griffith's *Seed in the Wind*, about racial tensions in a small southern town. Dismissed as a "dismal book, full of hackneyed situations and characters," it proposed that integration was punishment for the white man's sins against Negro women.[5] It dropped from sight like a stone, showing that a plotline revolving around race, justice, and civil rights was hardly enough to draw readers, even given the tenor of the times.

———

Nelle received a torrent of requests for interviews and book-signings. Sacks of fan mail arrived at Lippincott, her publisher. Truman wrote to friends, "Poor thing—she is nearly demented: says she gave up trying to answer her 'fan mail' when she recieved [*sic*] 62 letters in one day. I wish she could relax and enjoy it more: in this profession it's a long walk between drinks."[6]

Most of the letters lauded the book, but a few were angry. "In this day of mass rape of white women who are not morons, why is it that you young Jewish authors seek to whitewash the situation?" complained a reader. Nelle was tempted to reply, "Dear Sir or Madam, somebody is using your name to write dirty letters. You should notify the F.B.I." And she planned to sign it, "Harper Levy."[7]

One day, to escape the attention for a few hours, she used the excuse that Tay Hohoff was mad about cats to bring her an abandoned kitten with six toes on its forefeet. Nelle had found the kitten in the basement of her building, cuddled up to the furnace. She named it Shadrach, after the biblical character who endured Nebuchadnezzar's fiery furnace. After delivering it safely to the Hohoff sanctuary, a "beehive of books" scented with the aromas of tobacco and perfume, Nelle sank into a big comfortable chair and muttered, despite the early morning hour, "I *need* a drink. I'm supposed to be at an interview right now."[8] After she left, Tay and her husband had a good laugh about how their young friend was finding out that literary success was not always what it was cracked up to be.

In September 1960, with the book selling in the tens of thousands every week, Nelle retreated to Alabama for a book-signing at Capitol News and Book Company in Montgomery. Seated at a table next to a vase of white carnations, with a fresh-cut corsage pinned to her dress, she was the center of attention. Less a literary event than a combination celebration and reunion, the book-signing was an occasion where people "crowded into the bookstore because they saw her picture in the paper, wondered if she were kin to so and so, heard that her book was good, knew her at the University of Alabama, knew someone who used to know her somewhere or had read the book and enjoyed it and came to say so."[9]

Nearby was her father, 81-year-old Mr. Lee, looking very old as he watched quietly. His wife had been dead for almost a decade. (A. C. Lee himself would die in two years, still working at the firm of Barnett, Bugg & Lee.) His suit vests, once buttoned tightly over a healthy paunch, now hung loose. The knuckles of his right hand turned white when he pressed hard on the crook of his cane to rise from a chair and shake someone's hand.

But Nelle was grateful that her father had lived to witness this triumph. A perceptive newspaper reporter had remarked that *To Kill a Mockingbird* "is written out of Harper Lee's love for the South and Monroeville, but it is also the story of a father's love for his children, and the love they gave in return."[10] This came nearest to her true reason for writing the novel: it was a tribute to her father. The book's hero, the courageous but humble attorney Atticus Finch, was a portrait of A. C. Lee done in generous, loving strokes.

After a month's respite in Monroeville, Nelle returned to New York, hoping in vain that she could meet the demands the book was creating. But then, seeing there was no end in sight, she rushed off instead to the vacation house in rural Connecticut owned by her agents Annie Laurie and Maurice Crain. Truman, hearing of the effects of celebrity overtaking his friend, noted, "poor darling, she seems to be having some sort of happy nervous-breakdown."[11]

In December 1960, reviewers' year-end round-ups of the big books of the year ranked Harper Lee's first-ever novel with John Updike's *Rabbit, Run,* John O'Hara's *Sermons and Soda-Water,* James Michener's *Hawaii,* William Shirer's *The Rise and Fall of the Third Reich,* Allen Drury's *Advise and Consent,* Joy Adamson's *Born Free,* John Hersey's *The Child Buyer,* and John Knowles's *A Separate Peace.*

For someone like Nelle, who preferred solitude over parties, observing instead of participating, the onrush of instant celebrity resulting from *To Kill a Mockingbird* imposed a tremendous strain she hadn't expected. Somehow, in the space of a very short time, she had gone from having a private self that she could control to a public persona that she could not. Unlike Truman, for instance, who said, "I always knew that I wanted to be a writer and that I wanted to be rich and famous," Nelle didn't regard herself as an important person, and the attention being paid to her almost seemed to be happening to someone else.[12] (A revealing moment about her self-perception occurred during an interview with *Newsweek* in the lounge of New York's Algonquin Hotel. Catching sight of Irish playwright Brendan Behan walking by, she confessed, "I've always wanted to meet an author.")[13]

Just as long as the intense attention stayed primarily on the book, she could cope with it. Usually, her quick, folksy wit stood her in good stead during interviews. She was the first to poke fun at her heavy Alabama accent ("If I hear a consonant, I look around").[14] She deflected seriousness by claiming to be a Whig and believing "in Catholic emancipation and repeal of the Corn Laws," centuries-old issues in British politics.[15] Even her appearance was not off-limits, within reason; she admitted to being a little heavier than she would like to be (according to a friend, she put herself on a 1,000-calorie-a-day diet of "unpalatable goop").[16]

Periodically, she headed for Maurice and Annie Laurie's home for a rest, or her hometown. And of the two, Monroeville offered the safest harbor. Most reporters and interviewers, after studying maps of Alabama, where two-lane roads meandered like blue and black threads, opted to telephone the Lee residence instead. When the phone rang, often it was Alice who negotiated with the press. (Nelle was too much of a soft touch, in her opinion.)[17] The young author was grateful for her sister's determination that strangers not be allowed to interrupt the family's peace. The world and its demands could wait on the Lees' doorstep. Inside, Nelle liked to curl up with a book. Alice wouldn't even permit a television in the house to disturb the quiet.

When asked for more information about herself, Nelle responded coyly. At Huntingdon College, librarian Leo R. Roberts tried to compile facts about the former student for Nelle's admirers, who were clamoring to know more about the author. Roberts, probably a little frustrated by the scant information about Nelle in Huntingdon's archives, finally wrote to her in January 1961 requesting a summary of her background.

"I'm afraid a biographical sketch of me will be sketchy indeed; with the exception of M'bird, nothing of any particular interest to anyone has happened to me in my thirty-four years," she replied. After supplying a few details about her family, she deadpanned, "I was exposed to seventeen years of formal education in Monroeville schools, Huntingdon College, and the University of Alabama. If I ever learned anything, I've forgotten it."[18]

The evening after Nelle replied to Roberts at Huntingdon, Annie Laurie called from New York to say she had sold the movie rights to *To Kill a Mockingbird*.

The novel's skyrocketing sales had caught the attention of Hollywood almost immediately, and Annie Laurie, as Nelle's agent for dramatic rights, had been reviewing proposals from filmmakers.

Most offers were from small outfits and partnerships. Major studios passed on the book because *To Kill a Mockingbird* lacked the tried-and-true ingredients that attracted most movie audiences: shoot-'em-up action, a love story, danger, or a clear-cut "bad guy." In addition, the press had likened *To Kill a Mockingbird*'s young narrator, Scout, to preadolescent Frankie in Carson McCullers's *The Member of the Wedding*, and the film version of that novel had flopped. (The surface similarities of the two novels were not lost on McCullers, either, who commented acidly about Nelle to a cousin, "Well, honey, one thing we know is that she's been poaching on my literary preserves.")[19]

Annie Laurie also knew that in the long run working with a small company would be less threatening to the Lee family. She could close a film deal for the novel only if Alice and A. C. Lee approved of the people involved as much as Nelle. Whoever was chosen to turn the novel into a film had to come across as decent and trustworthy.

Her father and sister had arrived at the *To Kill a Mockingbird* party late, so to speak; but once it was clear that Nelle had achieved something grand, Mr. Lee and Alice—increasingly Alice as A. C. Lee's health declined—were taking over her affairs. Previously, when Nelle was working in New York full-time as an airline ticket agent during the 1950s and was hard-pressed for money, the Lees had allowed her to scrape along, probably figuring she would come to her senses eventually and return home. Then, against all odds, Nelle was suddenly famous. Now the family was in the spotlight and were trying to manage their prodigy.

A. C. Lee and Alice also hinted that they didn't believe this wild ride could last. Nelle had better be careful with her money.

"I never dreamed of what was going to happen. It was

somewhat of a surprise and it's very rare indeed when a thing like this happens to a country girl going to New York," Mr. Lee said when his daughter's novel simultaneously landed on the *New York Times* and *Chicago Tribune* bestseller lists. "She will have to do a good job next time if she goes on up," he continued, raising the issue of her possibly failing, even if he didn't mean it that way.[20]

Nelle's sister Louise was the least impressed of all by the attention given her sister's book and didn't think much of Nelle's talent, either. She told her son's teacher that *To Kill a Mockingbird* was just "ridiculous."[21]

So it was that when Annie Laurie wrote to the Lees about closing the deal on the motion picture rights, she acknowledged that Alice, as family spokesperson and Nelle's self-appointed manager, would have to be reckoned with every step of the way. "Dear Alice and Nelle," the letter began,

> [I tried] to keep in mind everything you said[,] Alice[,] about not getting any *cash* money for Nelle this year and not too much each succeeding year. . . . The sale is to Alan Pakula and Robert Mulligan, who are forming their own company to pro-duce together, with Bob Mulligan also directing. This is the real "prize" having him direct the Mockingbird picture. Alan is a good producer but he knew when he first talked to Nelle in our office, that he must have a sensitive director to work with him. We think that Bob Mulligan is just right for this picture.[22]

She was not overstating their good luck in closing with Alan Pakula and Bob Mulligan. As filmmakers, they were drawn to stories about character, life's tragic quality, and situations that were ripe for strong dramatization.

At first glance, Mr. Pakula would not give the impression of being the right man for the job of making a film about racial prejudice and a small southern town in the 1930s. Darkly handsome, the son of Polish immigrants, and a Yale graduate who dressed like a 1960s IBM salesman, Pakula was neat in ways that extended even to his film crews, insisting they pick up their cigarette butts after shooting on location. But he was also personable, warm, and conscientious.

Bob Mulligan had neither Pakula's charm nor his reserve. Sandy-haired, informal, and impulsive, Mulligan was born in the Bronx and studied briefly for the priesthood before enrolling at Fordham University. After serving with the Marines during World War II, he started at the bottom at CBS, as a messenger, but rose during the popularly nicknamed Golden Age of Television to become a director of live dramas. Unlike Pakula, however, who later moved into directing films with a social-political agenda, Mr. Mulligan would remain attracted to telling human-interest stories: *Love with a Proper Stranger* (1963); *Up the Down Staircase* (1967); *Summer of '42* (1971); and *The Man in the Moon* (1991).

Overall, the fit was good between the content of *To Kill a Mockingbird* and what Pakula and Mulligan wanted to do artistically. In the meantime, because Mulligan was still working on *The Spiral Road* (1962), a big-picture drama about colonialism in the tropics, Pakula made arrangements to visit Monroeville and "see Nelle about the 'creative side,'" as Annie Laurie put it, though he knew in advance he was auditioning for Alice and A.C.'s approval, too.

When he arrived in town in February 1961, the weather was overcast and rainy. But even if he had seen Monroeville under the best conditions, it wouldn't have changed his mind about using it as a possible location: "There is no Monroeville," Pakula wrote glumly to Mulligan, meaning that modernization over the last 30 years had rendered the town characterless. Except for the courthouse, which the citizenry was considering tearing down because a new, flat-roof, cinderblock version was on the drawing board, Monroeville was a mishmash of old and new. A façade for Scout's neighborhood would have to be built on a studio back lot, and the interior of the courthouse, which was not in good repair, would have to be measured and reconstructed on a Hollywood sound stage.

After spending several days getting to know the Lees, Pakula left for California, apparently having secured their approval for the ideas he and Mulligan had in mind for the film: "They want to give the movie the same approach that the book had," Alice said approvingly.[23]

———

The setting for fictional Maycomb that Pakula had expected to find had seemingly vanished. Where Truman's aunts' house had stood—the one belonging to Dill in the novel—was an empty lot. The Lees had moved to a brick ranch house across from the elementary school, and their trim white bungalow on South Alabama Avenue looked abandoned. The streets in town that had smoked with sour red dust on a hot day in the 1930s were smooth with asphalt now.

Just looking around, a visitor resting on one of the benches on the courthouse square might conclude that a film with a story like *To Kill a Mockingbird* was passé. How different times seemed from the days of lynch mobs and racist trials!

On the other hand, if anyone in Monroeville cared to notice—it was so much a part of life that no one would— blacks were not allowed to use the park or recreation facilities owned by Vanity Fair textiles, the largest industry in town, and there were separate water fountains marked WHITE and COLORED.

The long era of segregation and open racism was indeed dying—not gone, but dying—and *To Kill a Mockingbird* would help hasten its death. Some labeled the book just another of many cowardly blows falling on the South. In February 1961, a few days after newspapers announced the sale of the movie rights to the novel, an unsigned squib headed "Spreading Poison" appeared on the letters-to-the-editor page of the *Atlanta Journal-Constitution*: "That book 'To Kill a Mockingbird' is to be filmed. Thus another cruel, untrue libel upon the South is to be spread all over the nation. Another Alabama writer joins the ranks of traducers [traitors] of their homeland for pelf [ill-gotten money] and infamous fame."[24]

Yet the novel, and the issues it treated, was a sign of change that had been on the horizon for years. Perhaps that's why it wasn't criticized more often, because it was part of a series of ever-more-important events. The National Association for the Advancement of Colored People (NAACP) and the NAACP Legal Defense and Educational Fund had won *Brown v. Board of Education of Topeka* in 1954 before the U.S. Supreme Court, which ruled that segregation in the public schools was in itself unequal and thus unconstitutional. The following year, Rosa

Parks, a seamstress in Montgomery, Alabama, was arrested for disobeying a city law that required blacks to give up their seats to whites. The Montgomery bus boycott by black riders lasted 382 days, ending when the city abolished the bus law. It was the first organized mass protest by blacks in Southern history, and it thrust Martin Luther King, Jr., onto the national stage. The year *To Kill a Mockingbird* was published, 1960, black and white college students formed the Student Nonviolent Coordinating Committee (SNCC) to assist the civil rights movement with sit-ins, marches, boycotts, and demonstrations.

There was much trouble still ahead, but the days of overt social and legal inequities directed at blacks seemed numbered. In American culture, *To Kill a Mockingbird* would become like *Catch-22, One Flew Over the Cuckoo's Nest, On the Road, Soul on Ice,* and *The Feminine Mystique*—books that seized the imagination of the post–World War II generation—a novel that figured in changing "the system."

————

There was a lull in late spring 1961 with plans surrounding the movie. Pakula and Mulligan were anxious to get a commitment for the leading man, so they could move on to making a film distribution deal. The previous fall, Nelle had engaged in some star hunting on her own, thinking that a direct approach might entice an actor with a reputation for integrity suitable for Atticus. Through the William Morris Agency, she sent a note: "Dear Mr. [Spencer] Tracy, My agent has told me that your agent is sending you a copy of *To Kill a Mockingbird*. Frankly, I can't see anybody but Spencer Tracy in the part of 'Atticus.' "[25] The actor replied via an agent that he "could not read the book till he has finished his picture 'The Devil at Four O'clock.' He must study and concentrate at present." In March 1961, Maurice Crain wrote to Alice, "The latest development is that [entertainer] Bing Crosby very much wants to play Atticus. . . . He should be made to promise not to reverse his collar, not to mumble a single Latin prayer, not to burble a single note. . . . As for the Southern accent, he has been married for several years to a Texas girl and the accent is 'catching.' "[26]

———

On Monday, May 2, when *To Kill a Mockingbird* was in its 41st week as a bestseller and had sold nearly half a million copies, a phone rang in Annie Laurie and Maurice's offices. It was a friend of Annie Laurie's at a publishing house who wanted to speak to Nelle about hearsay from a reporter.

In California, Pakula had heard the same rumor and was excitedly calling his partner, Bob Mulligan.

When Mulligan answered, Pakula shouted, "We got it! We got it!"

"We got what?" asked Mulligan.

"The Pulitzer prize. Our book won it!"[27]

Nelle hardly dared believe the news until she received an official call. When she finally did hear from a spokesperson for the Pulitzer committee, she called Alice several times, who by now was becoming adept in the role of her sister's spokesperson and fielding phone calls from reporters. "Nelle was anxious to find out the local reaction," she said in response to questions.

"She still claims Monroeville as her home, and when she leaves, it is usually for business purposes" (a hint that Alice was still not reconciled to Nelle's living for months at a time in New York). "The whole town of Monroeville is amazed about the Pulitzer prize."[28]

The annual Pulitzer prizes in drama, letters, and music, created by newspaper publisher Joseph Pulitzer in a bequest to Columbia University, were worth only $500 at that time, but in terms of bringing artists' names to the public their influence was enormous.

A bookstore in New York City's Grand Central Station advertising that it carries To Kill a Mockingbird, *shortly after Nelle won the Pulitzer prize in May 1961. (Popular Library)*

Besieged by phone interviews that kept her pinned inside her agents' office for hours, Nelle resorted to modesty and humor as ways of modulating questions about herself. "I am as lucky as I can be. I don't know anyone who has been luckier."[29] She claimed that the effort to write the book had worn out three pairs of jeans. And about whether a movie was forthcoming based on the book, all she would say was that production was slated to begin in the fall.

Almost immediately, a second avalanche of correspondence began. "Snowed under with fan letters," wrote *Newsweek*, "Harper Lee is stealing time from a new novel-in-progress to write careful answers."[30]

It was the proverbial Cinderella story: from nowhere comes a young writer without benefit of grants, fellowships, or even an apprenticeship at a major newspaper or magazine, who produces, on her first try, a novel snapped up by three American book clubs: Reader's Digest Condensed Books, the Literary Guild, and the Book-of-the-Month Club. In addition, the British Book Society had selected it for its readers, and by the spring of 1961, translations were under way in France, Germany, Italy, Spain, the Netherlands, Denmark, Norway, Sweden, Finland, and Czechoslovakia.

Truman Capote, who craved winning the Pulitzer or the National Book Award, and hoped he would when *In Cold Blood* was finished, could barely conceal his envy in a letter to Kansas friends: "Well, and wasn't it fine about our dear little Nelle winning the Pulitzer Prize? She has swept the boards."[31]

And there was surely more to come from an author so promising. Nelle had written an essay, "Love—in Other Words," that appeared in the April issue of *Vogue* magazine. She told reporters that she had several short stories under way. She seemed to have talent and a work ethic that indicated a long career was just beginning.

In its first year, *To Kill a Mockingbird* sold more than 2,500,000 copies. Nelle wrote to friends in Mobile that W. S. Hoole, director of the University of Alabama libraries, "nearly fell over his size thirteens asking for the manuscript" for his archives, but she didn't give it to him for some reason.[32]

Maurice Crain, Annie Laurie Williams, and certainly Tay Hohoff couldn't wait for Nelle's second novel. In July 1961, a teasing note arrived at Nelle's apartment.

Dear Nelle: TOMORROW IS MY FIRST BIRTHDAY AND MY AGENTS THINK THERE SHOULD BE ANOTHER BOOK WRITTEN SOON TO KEEP ME COMPANY. DO YOU THINK YOU CAN START ONE BEFORE I AM ANOTHER YEAR OLD? We would be so happy if you would. [SIGNED] THE MOCKINGBIRD AND ANNIE LAURIE AND MAURICE CRAIN.[33]

To reporters asking the same question—what are your plans for a second book?—Nelle replied, "I guess I will have to quote Scarlett O'Hara on that. I'll think about that tomorrow."[34]

The remark was more than apt. Like the heroine from *Gone With the Wind*, for whom unpleasantness and hard decisions could always be put off until an eternal tomorrow, "tomorrow" would never come for Nelle Lee as an author. With her first novel, which became the most popular novel in American

Nelle in 1961, in the "Colored Only" gallery overlooking the courtroom of the Monroe County Courthouse, where her father once argued cases. (Donald Uhrbrock/Time & Life Pictures)

Harper Lee and her father at home on a summer day. Neighbors asked Mr. Lee to sign their copies of To Kill a Mockingbird "Atticus," which he gladly did. (Donald Uhrbrock/Time & Life Pictures)

literature in the twentieth century, and which readers in surveys rank as the most influential in their lives after the Bible, Nelle seemed poised to begin a career that would launch her into the annals of illustrious American writers.

Instead, almost from the day of its publication, *Mockingbird* took off and gradually left its author behind.

Chapter 8

"Oh, Mr. Peck!"

Oₙₑ COLD NIGHT IN EARLY JANUARY 1962, WEDNESDAY night services had just ended at the imposing First Baptist Church on Monroeville's town square when a stranger made his way up the front steps through the trickle of worshippers exiting the sanctuary. By his downcast and rough appearance, he appeared to be homeless.[1]

"May we help you?" asked one of the ushers.

"I'd like to see the reverend," came the gruff reply.

The usher assured the man that if he needed a meal or a place to stay, then that could be taken care of. No, that wasn't the problem, said the stranger. He needed to see the reverend. The usher, beckoning over a couple of gentlemen who were busy returning hymnals to the backs of pews, explained the situation. They agreed to accompany the visitor to Dr. L. Reed Polk's office.

Reverend Polk was just hanging up his vestments when the little group appeared on the threshold of his office. He thanked the ushers, invited the tall and rather well-built man in, and shut the door so they could have some privacy.

"What can I do for you?" asked Reverend Polk.

Looking up suddenly and extending his hand, the stranger said, "How do you do, sir? I'm Gregory Peck."

Peck was in town to meet the Lee family and observe the setting for the character he was going to play in the film version of *To Kill a Mockingbird*. The reason he had stopped at the First Baptist Church, he told Dr. Polk, was that he wanted to speak to someone who knew the town and its people. Dr. Polk had been the minister at First Baptist for more than 15 years. Peck apologized for the disguise, but he didn't want word to get around that he was visiting before he met the reverend. Dr. Polk was amused and flattered that Peck had come directly to him.

For the next hour, the two men talked about the town and about the man Peck was going to play. The actor asked for particulars about Mr. Lee's standing in the community, his thoughts and behaviors—anything that "set Mr. Lee apart" would be helpful. Dr. Polk stood up and demonstrated how Lee had a tendency to fumble with his penknife as he talked and how he paced back and forth. Peck watched intently, making mental notes about how he was going to embody Atticus Finch on the screen.

———

Actually, Gregory Peck had not been Universal Studios' first choice for the role. Rock Hudson was offered the part. But Pakula didn't want Mr. Hudson; he wanted Peck. The studio agreed that if the latter signed on, then it would provide part of the financing and see to the distribution. Pakula sent the actor a

Annie Laurie Williams had considerable experience with Hollywood when she sold the rights to Nelle's novel. One of the first books she successfully handled was Margaret Mitchell's Gone With the Wind. (Papers of Annie Laurie Williams, Columbia University)

Gregory Peck and Harper Lee took a brisk walk around Monroeville, Alabama, when he visited to meet her father, whom he would portray as Atticus Finch. (The Monroe Journal)

copy of the novel. "I got started on it," said Peck, "and of course I sat up all night and read straight through it. I understood that they wanted me to play Atticus and I called them at about eight o'clock in the morning and said, 'If you want me to play Atticus, when do I start? I'd love to play it.'"[2] Peck formed a production company called Brentwood Productions, which would be a three-way partnership with Pakula and Nelle. Peck, however, would have input into the film's casting, the development of the screenplay, and other creative decisions.

With Gregory Peck on board, the next piece of business was turning the novel into a screenplay. Pakula deferred to Nelle before approaching anyone else, but she wasn't interested. First, she was busy with a new novel, also set in the South. Working on it, she told a journalist, was like "building a house with matches."[3] The second reason was that she didn't mind if someone else pruned the book to fit a feature-length movie. She felt "indifference. After all, I don't write deathless prose." So Pakula turned to playwright Horton Foote. "I was asked to write the script," said Foote, "because the actor, producer, and Miss Lee were familiar with my writings."[4]

A stocky, soft-spoken Texan with blue eyes, Foote actually had very little experience as a film writer. The only other screenplay he'd written was a film-noir piece, *Storm Fear* (1955), the adaptation of a novel by Clinton Seeley.

When he was given the job of adapting *To Kill a Mockingbird*, he recognized a historical kinship with Nelle. His forebears had come from Alabama and Georgia in the early 1800s. Nevertheless, he worried about "despoiling the quality of the story" because "it's agonizing to try to get into someone else's psyche and to catch the essence of the work, yet knowing you can't be just literal about it. There has to be a point where you say, 'Well, the hell with it—I've got to do this job for another medium, and I've got to cut out this over-responsible feeling and roll my sleeves up and get to work.' "5

At Pakula's urging, Foote ratcheted up the drama by compressing the novel's three years into one. He also added a touch of backstory, too. "Harper never mentions the mother, and I was wondering how I could sneak in that emotional element. I remember as a boy my bedroom was right off the gallery on the porch and when I was supposed to be asleep I would hear things I was not supposed to hear from the adults. This was something I invented for the two children."6

Most important, he heightened the intensity of the novel's social criticism. Social protest, particularly about racial conditions in the South, receives more emphasis in Foote's screenplay than it does in Nelle's novel, a reflection of the civil rights movement's growing stronger. To underscore the film's seriousness, Foote removed some of Nelle's satire on "southernness." Gone are Aunt Alexandra's racist church ladies; Colonel Maycomb, admirer of Stonewall Jackson; and Miss Fischer, the barely competent first-grade teacher from north Alabama.

Foote also added a dab of love interest to the story. Miss Maudie from across the street appears at Atticus's breakfast table one morning, hinting that a romance might be in the offing. Nelle, on the other hand, preferred Atticus to be absolutely asexual—deaf, in fact, according to a political cartoon described in the novel, to the "yoo-hoo"s of ladies in the state capital who find the eligible attorney-legislator attractive.

In spite of the changes, Nelle later hailed Foote's screenplay.

"If the integrity of a film adaptation is measured by the degree to which the novelist's intent is preserved, Foote's screenplay should be studied as a classic."[7]

Director Bob Mulligan, on the other hand, wasn't so sure. "You know what your problem is," he told Alan Pakula, after reading Foote's work, "too often you lose the point of view of the children."[8] It was true, but Foote had chosen to thrust Atticus onto center stage at the expense of the children's coming-of-age story, believing the adult character would appeal to moviegoers.

A still more drastic change was contemplated. Before Peck had even read the screenplay, he wanted to drop the title *To Kill a Mockingbird*. Annie Laurie, who had assured Nelle that the novel's artistic integrity would be respected, was furious. "Don't believe any items you may see in the newspapers saying that Gregory Peck wants to change the title of *To Kill a Mocking-bird*," she wrote to George Stevens, managing editor at J. B. Lippincott. "He has been signed to play the part of Atticus, but has no right to say what the title of the picture will be. The change of title has been denied by Mulligan and Pakula in a column story in the *New York Times*."[9]

Nevertheless, Peck was the star of the film and had a considerable financial stake in it. Moreover, he had the support of Universal Studios in his back pocket. In ways that mattered, the film was more his than anybody else's.

After speaking to the Reverend Polk in his church office, Peck and his wife checked in at the ranch-style LaSalle Hotel in Monroeville. The following morning, Peck visited the Lees.

A. C. Lee was looking forward to meeting the actor, although he was feeling tired as a result of a mild heart attack. He'd never met a film star. For that matter, he'd never seen Gregory Peck in a movie. The two men sat in the living room getting to know each other, while Nelle and Alice had to keep shooing away neighbors who were trying to peek in through the picture window. Peck got the impression that the elderly lawyer "was much amused by the invasion of these Hollywood types. He looked on us with benign amusement."[10] They got along together well.

After an hour or so of conversation, Nelle offered to take Peck on a short tour of the square with a stop-off for lunch. The weather was brisk and overcast, but Peck, dressed in only a lightweight suit, gamely followed Nelle, who was wearing a parka, jeans, white socks, and sneakers, around town until they arrived at the Wee Diner.

The Wee Diner was two Montgomery buses joined at a 45-degree angle, head to rear, creating a triangular courtyard effect. The intersection served as the entrance. To rustle up customers, owner Frank Meigs put a chopped onion on the grill and turned on the exhaust fan, a welcome smell to Nelle and Peck on such a chilly January day. They took one of the booths and ordered.

Suddenly through the door came Wanda Biggs, the official hostess for the Welcome Wagon. She had been tracking them all over town, she said breathlessly. On behalf of the Chamber of Commerce, she presented Gregory Peck with a basket of gifts and coupons for newcomers. "He was as polite and kind a man I had ever met," she later told everyone. "He asked if I would mind taking it to his wife across the street at the hotel. That he would like for me to meet her. I did and found her to be equally as warm and friendly. They were just our kind of folks."[11]

Nelle and Peck's final stop after the Wee Diner was the home of Charles Ray Skinner. The production crew arranged to meet them there because they wanted to photograph what servants' quarters looked like in an older home. Peck made small talk with Skinner about the spacious kitchen, including that he'd never had a real down-home Southern meal.

Probably as a result of that remark, by seven thirty that evening, the lobby of the LaSalle Hotel was jammed with ladies bringing covered dishes. Peck left a message at the front desk expressing his thanks and asked that items for him be left for him to pick up. Not to be denied, teenager Martha Jones and a friend pushed through to the receptionist and asked which room Mr. and Mrs. Peck were staying in. She told them huffily that the Pecks were not in at present. The two girls got in their car and drove around town on a scavenger hunt until they spotted Nelle's car outside the Monroe Motor Court. Door by door they listened in. Finally, hearing voices, they knocked on one, and were confronted by Nelle, who was obviously not amused.

"Martha Louise Jones, what are you doing here?"

"I was just hoping I could get Mr. Peck's autograph."

Beyond Nelle, Martha could see Mr. Peck, his wife, and Mr. Lee.

"Well, we're busy now. You just go on home," ordered Nelle, and began to shut the door.

"Hold on, Nelle," Peck interrupted. "I'll be glad to give the young ladies my autograph." Star struck, the two fans offered him damp scraps of paper. He signed both and then bid the girls a gracious good night.[12]

The following morning, until it was time to leave, Mr. and Mrs. Peck didn't venture outside the LaSalle Hotel lest they send the town into a second uproar. Frank Meigs sent over breakfast from the Wee Diner, and later Peck sent him a hand-written note expressing his gratitude.

Production on the film was scheduled to begin in early February in Hollywood, and Nelle had been invited to attend. But she had also promised Truman she would go with him to Kansas again after Christmas. So during the middle of January— two weeks after Peck had left Monroeville—she was back in Garden City, once again as Truman's "assistant researchist," though by now her profile in town was higher than his.

"It was pretty dicey for Nelle, as she was known by local people who had come to like her very much," said Dolores Hope.

She was always very protective of Capote and made sure the limelight was on him most of the time. She was quick to divert mention of the Pulitzer Prize back to Capote. She also gave him credit for his help and encouragement. My impression of the Pulitzer time is that people who had come to know Truman here in Kansas just had a gut feeling that he would have his nose out of joint about it. Nelle knew him so well and she was anything but an attention-getter herself. In fact, she shunned it. She was the exact opposite of Truman, being more interested in others than she was in herself.[13]

Her stay was necessarily brief, however, because filming was slated to begin in a few weeks. Consequently, at the end of the first week of February, she boarded the Super Chief in Garden City, having finished helping Truman, and continued on to Los Angeles. Total sales of her book, hardback and paperback, were approaching four and a half million.

Casting had been completed just in the nick of time, with some of the roles settled on just weeks before shooting began. Pakula and Mulligan preferred faces audiences wouldn't recognize, "to retain the sense of discovery, which is so important in the novel," Pakula said.[14] They turned to character actors from films, Broadway professionals—unfamiliar then to most filmgoing audiences—and, for the roles of the children, complete unknowns. Another newcomer was Robert Duvall, who had impressed Foote when Duvall gave a first-rate performance in Foote's drama *The Midnight Caller* at the Neighborhood Playhouse in New York. To prepare for the role of Boo Radley, Duvall stayed out of the sun for six weeks and dyed his hair blond, thinking it would give him an angelic look.

The competition for the role of Tom Robinson was down to two actors: Brock Peters and James Earl Jones. Peters badly wanted the part because his career seemed to be slipping into a rut of playing villains. "Well, of course, I was scared out of my wits," he remembered. "I didn't know how to present myself in order to get this coveted prize. I went into the meeting—it was in a building at Park Avenue and 57th Street and I tried not to appear frightened but I wanted to look cool and calm and still suggest the character of Tom Robinson, and do that dressed in a suit."15 He got the part, and a few days before filming began, Peck called to congratulate him. Peters was so surprised he didn't know what to say at first. "I worked over the years in many, many productions, but no one ever again called me to welcome me aboard, except perhaps the director and the producer, but not my fellow actor-to-be."16

The part of Bob Ewell, the poor white who accuses Tom Robinson, was still open when actor James Anderson met with Bob Mulligan. Raised in Alabama, Anderson told Mulligan with conviction, "I know this man." Mulligan believed he did, but he also had to confront Anderson with his reputation for drinking, fighting, and not showing up to sets. He told Anderson to come back in three days (probably to see whether he would be on time and sober). When Anderson arrived, Mulligan laid it on the line: "I want you to be in this movie but you and I are going to have to have a clear understanding. And you're going to have to take my hand and shake it. If you do, you have to promise me that you will be sober, that you will be on time, that you will not cause trouble for me or for anyone. And that you will do honor to this script. He said, 'I understand.' He put out his hand and shook mine, and he kept his word."17

The role of Jem went to 13-year-old Phillip Alford, a child with practically no acting experience who auditioned only because his parents promised him a day off from school. Hundreds of children competed for the roles of the Finch children, including nine-year-old Mary Badham, who was selected for

Director Robert Mulligan encouraged Phillip Alford, Mary Badham, and John Megna to play together. Then he would move the cameras in quietly and tell them to begin saying their lines. (PhotoFest)

the part of Scout. She was feisty and frank, a good match for her character. When a reporter commented, "You're a very little girl for your age," she replied, "You'd be little, too, if you drank as much coffee as I do."[18]

By coincidence, Phillip and Mary were Birmingham natives who lived four blocks apart. The Alfords were, however, working-class people, and the Badhams could afford a black nanny to help raise Mary. The part of the Finches' next-door neighbor went to nine-year-old John Megna, who had recently appeared in the Broadway hit *All the Way Home*, based on James Agee's Pulitzer prize–winning novel, *A Death in the Family*. "John looked up to me like a big brother," Phillip later said, and the two boys formed a pact to hate Mary.[19]

The directors had already arranged to shoot many of the scenes on sound stages at the Revue Studios, but that left the question about what to do for exterior scenes, since Monroeville no longer resembled a Depression-era Southern town. Alexander Golitzen, a former architect and the film's co–art director, studied sketches and photographs of Monroeville until he came up with an idea. Some of the older homes resembled the clapboard cottages that were disappearing from the outskirts of Los Angeles. Golitzen suggested to his colleague Henry Bumstead that they get tips from wrecking companies on houses slated for demolition. Near Chavez Ravine, where a new baseball park for the Los Angeles Dodgers was nearing completion, they found a dozen condemned cottage-style houses. For practically nothing they hauled the frames to the set. Sometimes known as "shotgun hall" houses because they have a center hall, with all the rooms off to the left or right, they were popular everywhere in the United States during the first 30 years or so of the 20th century. For a quarter of the cost of building them from scratch on the set, the relocated houses were placed on either side of a recreated Alabama street, with porches, shutters, and gliders (seat swings) added for a touch of Southern flair.[20] When Nelle arrived on the set in early February, she was dazzled by the illusion.

On February 12, principal photography began. Until now, Nelle had been harboring some doubts about Mr. Peck's suitability for the role. "The first time I met him was at my home in Alabama. . . . I'd never seen Mr. Peck, except in films, and when I saw him at my home I wondered if he'd be quite right for the part." But that was without seeing him in character. "[T]he first glimpse I had of him was when he came out of his dressing room in his Atticus suit. It was the most amazing transformation I had ever seen. A middle-aged man came out. He looked bigger, he looked thicker through the middle. He didn't have an ounce of makeup, just a 1933-type suit with a collar and a vest and a watch and chain. The minute I saw him I knew everything was going to be all right because he *was* Atticus."[21]

After two whirlwind days in Hollywood, she had to leave on family business. It was too bad she couldn't have stayed to see the courtroom scenes. To film them, scenarists constructed a sound-stage set built to look exactly like the interior of the courthouse in Monroeville, based on painstaking measurements. Ironically, one of the novel's major themes is tolerance, but a production assistant kept reassembling the extras for the trial by shouting, "All the colored atmosphere upstairs; all the white atmosphere downstairs." Brock Peters had a word with him, and the call was changed to "Downstairs atmosphere in, please; balcony atmosphere upstairs, please." Because of the values of the times, Phillip, Mary, and John were not allowed to

Producer Alan Pakula and Nelle Lee watch scenes on the set of To Kill a Mockingbird. (AP photo)

Gregory Peck points out something in the script to Nelle. (Corbis)

attend the filming of the courtroom scenes, even though they appear to be watching from the courtroom gallery. For children that age, listening to a trial about rape and incest, even a fictional one, was considered inappropriate.

During the trial, Brock Peters delivered one of the most memorable performances in the entire film. For two weeks of rehearsals and filming, he was required to break down on the witness stand, begin to weep, and then make a dignified attempt to try to stifle his sobs. By the end of this slow disintegration, his self-respect has to gain hold again and turn into barely suppressed rage at being falsely accused. Bob Mulligan coached him until "Once we were on track I needed to go only to the places of pain, remembered pain, experienced pain and the tears would come, really at will." Peters later called those two intense weeks "my veil of tears."[22] Peck found it difficult to watch Peters because the actor's performance was so affecting.

Between Gregory Peck and James Anderson, however, there was no love lost. To begin with, Anderson would speak only to Mulligan for some reason. Peck tried to make a suggestion about one of their scenes; Anderson snarled back, "You don't show me *shit*!"[23] Second, he was a Method actor, meaning that he tried to remain in character at all times, which in this case was a violent man. In the struggle with Jem Finch near the end of the film, Mr. Anderson yanked Phillip out of the camera frame by his hair.[24]

———

In April, after a month of filming, word reached the set that Nelle had returned to Monroeville just in time because her family needed her again. At age 82, A. C. Lee died early in the morning on Palm Sunday, April 15, 1962.

Of his daughter Nelle, A. C. Lee had said, "It was my plan for her to become a member of our law firm—but it just wasn't meant to be. She went to New York to become a writer."[25] It was typical of him that he tended to think the best of others, including his headstrong daughter, who had proven him wrong about her choice to drop out of law school and write fiction instead. He believed that people are basically good, capable of improving, and as eager as the next person for a better future.

Worth pointing out, however, is that A. C. Lee himself only gradually rose to the moral standards of Atticus during his life. Though more enlightened than most, he was no saint, no prophet crying in the wilderness with regard to racial matters. In many ways, he was typical of his generation, especially about issues surrounding integration. Like most of his contemporaries, he believed that the current social order, segregation, was natural and created harmony between the races. For him, it was a point not even worth discussing that blacks and whites were different. As the Bible said, "In my Father's house are many mansions." That divine structure's great roof covered all humanity. Hence, blacks deserved consideration and charity as fellow creatures of God; and the law should protect them. But they were not the same as white people; and for that simple reason—to continue the biblical metaphor—they did not need to be in the same room with whites.

And it may surprise admirers of Atticus Finch that the man he was modeled after did not believe that a church pulpit was the proper place for preaching about racial equity. He insisted that the mission of the Methodist Church, where his family had worshipped for generations, was to bring people to salvation, *not* to promote social justice.[26] On this point he was in agreement with Methodist pastor G. Stanley Frazier, an outspoken segregationist in Montgomery who believed that the church should bring souls to God, and not ensnare them in passing social problems.

But A. C. Lee changed his views during the remainder of the 1950s. And Nelle watched as her father, formerly a conservative on matters of race and social progress, became an advocate for the rights of blacks.

Part of the reason for his change of mind was the influence of events that no thoughtful American in the 1950s could ignore. In 1954, two white men murdered Emmett Till, a 14-year-old black visiting Mississippi from his home in Chicago because he had whistled at a white woman. The killers were acquitted, and then bragged about their crime to the media. Two years later, Autherine Lucy, a black student, attempted to enroll at Nelle's alma mater, the University of Alabama, but racist violence on the campus for three days forced her to flee.

A contest of warring principles was gearing up in the South, and a civic-minded man such as A. C. Lee could not fail to recognize it happening in his own backyard. In 1959 in Monroeville, the Ku Klux Klan forced the cancellation of the annual Christmas parade by threatening to kill any members of the all-black Union High School band who marched. The morning after the parade was canceled, A. C. Lee walked into the store owned by A. B. Blass, noting that the store's exterior was covered with racist graffiti. As president of Kiwanis, Blass had made the decision to call off the parade for safety's sake. "Mr. Lee came down to our store from his office and knowing what we had done put his hand on my shoulder," said Blass, "looked me in the eye and said, 'Son, you did the right thing.' "[27]

By the time *To Kill a Mockingbird* was published, A. C. Lee counted himself an activist in defending the civil rights of blacks. In 1962, while a reporter was interviewing Nelle in Monroeville, he and Alice stopped by on their way to the offices of Barnett, Bugg & Lee. The 81-year-old A. C. Lee interrupted to speak earnestly about the importance of reapportioning the voting district to provide fairer representation for black voters. "It's got to be done," he said.[28]

Though this was not a complete reversal of his belief that the church should stay out of nonreligious affairs, it was clear that racial equity had become a matter of conscience for A. C. Lee, and so it had entered the realm of moral judgment where he had to confront what he believed about humanity. Like his persona, Atticus Finch, he came to believe "You never really understand a person until you consider things from his point of view . . . until you climb into his skin and walk around in it."[29]

Influencing him, too, was his daughter Alice, more progressive in outlook in matters concerning race than he was. At a critical moment in reorganizing the Methodist Church, for instance, Alice took her stand.

During a meeting in the mid-1960s of the Church's Alabama–West Florida Conference, one of the few regional holdouts against integrating black Methodists with whites, a "committee report concerning the problems of our racially divided church and society had come to the floor," said Reverend Thomas Butts of Monroeville. "Amendments had been made, and debate had started. The advocates of continued

racism were poised and ready to try to drag the church deeper
into institutional racism, but before their titular leader could
get the floor, a wee woman from Monroeville got the attention
of the presiding officer of the conference."

For years, Alice had been impatiently waiting for such an
opportunity. A simple motion had been made and seconded to
combine the black and white churches. The floor was open for
debate. Taking the floor microphone, recalled Reverend Butts,
Alice made "her maiden speech to the Alabama–West Florida
Conference of the Methodist Church. Her speech electrified the
seven- or eight-hundred delegates. It consisted of five words.
She said: 'I move the previous question,' and sat down. The
conference applauded enthusiastically and voted overwhelm-
ingly to support her motion, and then proceeded to adopt the
committee report without further debate. The advocates of
racism were left holding their long-prepared speeches. Miss
Alice became the hero of the conference and from that day the
enemy of the racists."[30]

On Easter Sunday, a week after his death, the *Montgomery
Advertiser* wished for more men like A. C. Lee to come to the
aid of the South and help pour oil on the roiling waters of the
civil rights movement and its opponents: white supremacists.

Harper Lee, as is the case with most writers of fiction,
says that the father in her book, Atticus Finch, isn't exactly
her father. But she told John K. Hutchens of the *New York
Herald Tribune* book section the other day that Atticus Finch

was very like her father "in character and—the South has a
good word for this—in 'disposition.'"

What makes Atticus Finch or Amasa Coleman Lee, thus
a remarkable man? He was a teacher of his own children, a
small-town citizen who thought about things and tried to be
a decent Christian human being. He succeeded.

... Many Southern individuals and families with the
Lee-Finch family principles have not asserted themselves and
offset another image of the Deep South.

This may be an appropriate thought for this Easter Day.
But if it is appropriate, let the individual say. The Lee family,
and the Finch, is one of great independence. Amasa Coleman
Lee, so evidently a great man, voted Democratic until the
mid-30s, then independently. Said a daughter, "We have a
great tendency to vote for individuals, instead of parties. We
got it from him."

Indeed, was and is the Lee-Finch family so unusual?
Could Amasa Coleman Lee, in his care, responsibility and
sense of justice, have been so unusual and served so long in
the Alabama Legislature, or so long edited a county newspaper in the deep south of this Deep South state?

There are many "likenesses" of Atticus Finch. They are
far too silent.[31]

After her father's death, Nelle buried herself in writing.
"Not a word from Nelle," Truman wrote to Alvin and Marie
Dewey on May 5, "though I read in a magazine that she'd
'gone into hiding; and was hard at work on her second
novel.'"[32]

Principal shooting on *To Kill a Mockingbird* had ended May 3, and the picture wrapped in early June 1962. During the five months of production, Phillip Alford, in the role of Jem, had grown from four foot eleven to five foot three, and his costumes had to be altered several times. Also, his voice was beginning to change. The final scene to be filmed was the one outside the jail when Atticus is protecting his client from a lynch mob and the children unexpectedly intervene. Mary, who didn't want the film to end, kept deliberately flubbing her lines over and over, until her mother pulled her aside and told her that Los Angeles traffic would be a nightmare if she made everybody stay any longer. Chastened, she said her lines correctly, then Peck, whom the children loved to spray with squirt guns, stepped back. From overhead, the lighting crew poured buckets of water on Scout, Jam, and Dill.

Peck said he felt good about how the shooting went. "It seemed to just fall into place without stress or strain."[33] He was not pleased, however, when he saw the rough cut of the picture. In a memo to his agent, George Chasin, and to Universal executive Mel Tucker, dated June 18, 1962, he itemized 44 objections to the way his character was presented. In sum, the children appeared too often, in his opinion, and their point of view diminished the importance of Atticus. "Atticus has no chance to emerge as courageous or strong. Cutting generally seems completely antiheroic where Atticus is concerned, to the point where he is made to be wishy-washy. Don't understand this approach." But Pakula and Mulligan had taken the precaution of stipulating in the beginning that they would make the final cut, which kept them, not the studio, in control of the editing.

After reviewing Peck's memo, Mulligan and Pakula made another pass at editing the film, but the star still wasn't satisfied. In a second memo to Tucker, on July 6, Peck wrote, "I believe we have a good character in Atticus, with some humor and warmth in the early stages, and some good emotion and conflict in the trial and later on. . . . In my opinion, the picture will begin to look better as Atticus' story line emerges, and the children's scenes are cut down to proportion."[34] More footage fell to the cutting room floor, including whole scenes of the children. Pakula said later, "It just tore my heart out to lose the sequence [where Jem reads aloud to Mrs. Dubose, who is dying]."[35]

In the end, Peck positioned himself firmly and prominently at the center of the film. Only about 15 percent of the novel is devoted to Tom Robinson's rape trial, whereas in the film, the running time is more than 30 percent of a two-hour film.

Meanwhile, Nelle continued to work on her follow-up to *To Kill a Mockingbird*, because the pressure was on for a repeat performance. In August, Truman wrote to the Deweys, "As for Nelle—what a rascal! Actually, I know she is trying very hard to get a new book going. But she loves you dearly, so I'm sure you will be the first to hear from her when she *does* reappear."[36]

Truman hinted that he knew how Nelle was coming on her new book, but apparently she didn't confide in him about it. "I can't tell you much about Nelle's new book," he wrote to a friend. "It's a novel, and quite short. But she is *so* secretive."[37]

In any case, she couldn't have been devoting much time to it, because publicity demands having to do with the upcoming release of the film were keeping her busy.

On Christmas Day 1962, *To Kill a Mockingbird* premiered in Hollywood. At a buffet supper afterward, film celebrities who had attended the screening—Rock Hudson, Gregory Peck, Natalie Wood, and Paul Newman, among others—offered Nelle their congratulations. "It's a fantastically good motion picture," she said happily to the press, "and it remained faithful to the spirit of the book. It is unpretentious. Nothing phony about it."[38]

First Lady Jackie Kennedy arranged for a private showing in Washington, D.C., in early January for one of her charities. Alan Pakula proudly showed it to several senators and Supreme Court judges, but he ended up with the wrong print, "a study in grays—no black and white resonance. It was one of the worst nights of my life."[39]

On Valentine's Day 1963, the film opened in New York City. Nelle soldiered on through another public appearance, having given her word that she would. Audiences lined up around the block. Reviewers by and large praised the film as entertainment, though some of the more perceptive identified problems created by the differences between the novel and the script.

"The trial weighed upon the novel, and in the film, where it is heavier, it is unsupportable. The narrator's voice returns at the end, full of warmth and love . . . but we do not pay her the same kind of attention any more. We have seen that outrageous trial, and we can no longer share the warmth of her love," wrote *Newsweek*.[40] Bosley Crowther in the *New York Times* pointed out, "It is, in short, on the level of adult awareness of right and wrong, of good and evil, that most of the action in the picture occurs. And this detracts from the camera's observation of the point of view of the child. . . . [I]t leaves the viewer wondering precisely how the children feel. How have they really reacted to the things that affect our grown-up minds?"[41]

Brendan Gill, writing for *The New Yorker*, disliked that the film's resolution, Bob Ewell's death, was no more defensible than it was in the novel: "In the last few minutes of the picture, whatever intellectual and moral content it may be said to have contained is crudely tossed away in order to provide a 'happy' ending. . . . The moral of this can only be that while ignorant rednecks mustn't take the law into their own hands, it's all right for *nice* people to do so."[42]

Nelle was unfazed. "For me, Maycomb is there, its people are there: in two short hours one lives a childhood and lives it with Atticus Finch, whose view of life was the heart of the novel."[43]

———

The Alabama premiere took place on March 15, with many shows sold out in advance. Two weeks later, the film arrived in Monroeville, and Nelle was there to witness the reaction. A full-page ad in the *Monroe Journal*, paid for by local businesses, trumpeted, "We Are Proud of Harper Lee . . . and Her Masterpiece! We Would Like to Share with Her These Moments of Artistic Triumph!" Reserved-seat tickets were on sale by March 17 at the theater box office or by mail order: $1.00 for adults and $0.50 for children. The first five customers who brought in a live mockingbird would receive $10 apiece.

Dorothy and Taylor Faircloth drove over from Atmore on a clear and cool night to see the movie. "You were really fortunate to get tickets. It was a fantastic event for a small town like Monroeville."[44] Also in the audience was Joseph Blass, who, as a teenager, had caddied for Nelle's father. "Mr. Lee did not look much like Peck in the movie, although Peck, who had spent time with Mr. Lee, copied some of his mannerisms in a way that was almost eerie to those of us who knew him."[45]

When the final credit ended, there was no applause. Few people said anything until they reached the lobby. "At that time in the South, everybody seemed to be divided. You were either a liberal or a racist. And when the movie ended, the discussion afterwards went along those lines."[46] The film was held over a week. Nelle posed for a photo under the marquee with some Monroeville dignitaries, squinting in the springtime daylight, but obviously beaming.

The movie was the object of enjoyment and praise, but judging from its premiere in Birmingham, Alabama, at least, it didn't seem to prick people's consciences. When it opened on April 3 at the Melba Theater, "huge crowds jammed the street . . . to catch a glimpse of the movie's two child stars: Birmingham natives Mary Badham and Phillip Alford," writes Jonathan S. Bass in *Blessed Are the Peacemakers.* At the same time the Melba Theater was filled with appreciative audiences, the Southern Christian Leadership Conference had organized thousands of black children for a civil rights march in the city. Police carried them off to jail in buses. When there was no more room, Police Chief "Bull" Connor ordered that police dogs and fire hoses be turned on the demonstrators. The torrent of water sent small children skidding down the street.[47]

By spring of 1963, the film version of *To Kill a Mockingbird* had been nominated for eight Academy Awards, including Best Picture, Best Director, Best Supporting Actress (Mary Badham), Best Black-and-White Cinematography, and Best Music Score—Substantially Original.

On awards night, April 8, Nelle went to a friend's house in Monroeville to watch the presentations. She didn't own a television because "it interferes with my work." Horton Foote won the Best Adapted Screenplay Oscar, and the team of Art Directors/Set Decorators for *To Kill a Mockingbird* also received the top honor. Some days before the ceremony, Nelle had sent Gregory Peck her father's pocket watch, engraved, "To Gregory from Harper." Now, as he sat in Hollywood waiting for the envelope to be opened and the announcement made of who had been voted Best Actor, Peck clutched the watch. When Sophia Loren read his name as the winner, he strode onto the stage with the watch still in his hand. One of the first people he thanked was Harper Lee.

She cried "tears of joy."[48]

A few days later, Truman returned to Monroeville from Switzerland to visit his aunt Mary Ida Carter. About 40 people attended a little party at the Carter home for both Truman and Nelle. But most of the attention, Truman couldn't help but notice, went to Nelle.[49]

Chapter 9

The Second Novel

AFTER THE END OF THE PUBLICITY FOR *To Kill a Mockingbird,* Nelle was free now to work practically as much as she liked on her next novel. Splitting her time between New York and Monroeville, she bent to the task of trying to write regularly. Requests for personal appearances and speeches were still pouring in, but she decided since "I'm in no way a lecturer or philosopher, my usefulness there is limited." At a dinner given in her honor at the University of Alabama, she warned her hosts to expect a "two-word speech," and that if she felt talkative, she might add "very much."[1]

Even in Monroeville, however, demands on her time were hard to escape. "I've found I can't write on my home grounds. I have about 300 personal friends who keep dropping in for a cup of coffee. I've tried getting up at 6, but then all the 6 o'clock risers congregate."[2] To get away by herself, she went to the golf course, forgiving her neighbors for their trespasses on her privacy. "Well, they're Southern people, and if they know you are working at home they think nothing of walking right in for a cup of coffee. But they wouldn't dream of interrupting you at golf."[3] She liked to spend the hours on the golf course thinking about her novel. "Playing golf is the best way I know to be alone and still be doing something. You hit a ball, think, take a walk. I do my best thinking walking. I do my dialog, talking it out to myself."[4]

She had to know at least two chapters ahead what characters were going to do and say before she could make any progress. Even so, she was a slow writer. Her method was to "finish a page or two, put them aside, look at them with a fresh eye, work on them some more, then rewrite them all over again."[5]

As 1963 neared an end, Alice did a rough estimate of her sister's income and taxes. Nelle "nearly flipped," Alice wrote Annie Laurie about the tax implications, "and she worried terribly for a short while, then she took off to the golf course and had a good time."[6]

———

In the spring, Nelle returned to New York. She was eager to continue her stays with Annie Laurie and Maurice at the Old Stone House in Connecticut, where she could be with friends but also left alone when she needed to work. "I have a place where I don't know anybody and nobody knows me. I'm not going to tell, because somebody would know."[7] Although writing "has its own rhythm," she said, it was "the loneliest work there is."[8]

She also had to be back in New York because Truman needed her help with the final phases of *In Cold Blood*. For more than four years, he had been laboring on the manuscript. His

Nelle at the Old Stone House in Connecticut, where she often went to work on her second novel. That book never appeared. (Papers of Annie Laurie Williams, Columbia University)

childish handwriting filled more than a dozen school notebooks, every paragraph double-spaced and written in pencil. The work continued while he made return trips to Garden City, sometimes accompanied by Nelle, and to the Kansas State Penitentiary to interview Perry Smith and Richard Hickock on death row.

Most of the book was finished by 1964, but appeals by the killers' attorneys forced the case upward through the legal system, even to the U.S. Supreme Court. Truman wrote to his publisher, Bennett Cerf at Random House, "please bear in mind that I *cannot* really finish the book until the case has reached its legal termination, either with the execution of Perry and Dick (the probable ending) or a commutation of sentence (highly *un*likely). . . . Nevertheless, it is the most difficult writing I've ever done (my God!) and an excruciating thing to live with day in and day out on and on—but it *will* be worth it: I *know*."[9]

Of the two possible outcomes, Truman knew that the most satisfactory dramatic ending would be execution by hanging. KBI detective Harold Nye, who had pursued the killers all over the West, wouldn't settle for anything less. "I'm not really bloodthirsty," he wrote to Truman, "but I will never feel the case is closed until I see that pair drip [*sic*] through the hole."[10]

Truman had written all but the final chapter when he stopped off in Topeka to see Nye at his home. It was then that the detective learned that Truman could be ruthless—not about justice, but about his art, his career, his reputation. It seemed as if the process of reporting and writing the book had transformed him into a person who was, more than ever, completely self-centered and willing to exploit any of his friends in his own self-aggrandizing quest for fame and fortune.

While they were talking about the case and the final stages of the book, Nye remarked, "Well, Nelle will certainly play a part in all this."

"*No*," Truman said emphatically, "she was just there."

That response startled Nye. "As well as they knew each other," he said, looking back, "there is no reason not to give some credit to her."[11]

While she was in New York in March 1964, Nelle gave one of her last interviews, which also happened to be her best. She appeared on Roy Newquist's evening radio show, *Counterpoint*, on WQRX in New York. A genial and engaging man, Newquist had the ability to put people at ease. And Nelle, normally given to bantering with reporters and deflecting personal questions, opened up as she never had about her work and her aims as a writer.[12]

She described herself to Newquist as someone who "*must* write. . . . I like to write. Sometimes I'm afraid that I like it too much because when I get into work I don't want to leave it. As a result I'll go for days and days without leaving the house or wherever I happen to be. I'll go out long enough to get papers and pick up some food and that's it. It's strange, but instead of hating writing I love it too much." Newquist asked her to name the contemporary writers she admired most. At the top of her list she put her friend Truman Capote.

"There's probably no better writer in this country today than Truman Capote. He is growing all the time. The next thing coming from Capote is not a novel—it's a long piece of reportage, and I think it is going to make him bust loose as a novelist. He's going to have even deeper dimension to his work. Capote, I think, is the greatest craftsman we have going."

About her own ambition as a writer, she expressed a desire to write more and better novels in the vein of *To Kill a Mockingbird*.

> I hope to goodness that every novel I do gets better and
> better, not worse and worse. I would like, however, to do one

thing, and I've never spoken much about it because it's such a personal thing. I would like to leave some record of the kind of life that existed in a very small world. I hope to do this in several novels—to chronicle something that seems to be very quickly going down the drain. This is small-town middle-class southern life as opposed to the Gothic, as opposed to *Tobacco Road*, as opposed to plantation life.

As you know, the South is still made up of thousands of tiny towns. There is a very definite social pattern in these towns that fascinates me. I think it is a rich social pattern. I would simply like to put down all I know about this because I believe that there is something universal in this little world, something decent to be said for it, and something to lament in its passing.

And then she added a remark that set the bar high for herself—perhaps too high, in hindsight—but one that seemed plausible for a writer who had already written one of the most popular books since World War II.

"In other words," she said, "all I want to be is the Jane Austen of south Alabama."[13]

———

In January 1965, Nelle was involved in a terrible kitchen accident. She "burned herself very badly, especially her right hand. It seems some sort of pan caught fire and exploded," Truman said.[14] Friends called and sent cards from New York and Kansas as word spread that the accident was serious and she was in the hospital.

With her hand wrapped in white gauze from her fingers to her forearm, she was limited to reading and answering correspondence with Alice's help. It would be months before a doctor could fully determine whether she would need plastic surgery. Perhaps because she was out of action at the typewriter, Nelle accepted an invitation of the sort that she would normally refuse on the grounds that she was "in no way a lecturer or philosopher."

Colonel Jack Capp, course director of English 102 at the United States Military Academy at West Point, had added *To Kill a Mockingbird* to the freshman syllabus. With the permission of the department head, he ventured to invite Nelle to address the freshman class of cadets. There was a precedent for this: three years earlier, William Faulkner had accepted a token honorarium of $100 for speaking there. "She was interested," recalled Colonel Capp, "but deferred acceptance until we could meet her in New York to discuss details. Mid-morning on the appointed day, Mike Cousland, a well-featured, mannerly bachelor major and I went to Harper's pied-à-terre in Manhattan, a small apartment on the upper East Side."[15] After a nice get-to-know-you chat, a date was suggested and Nelle agreed. Then she insisted they go to Sardi's for lunch. After which, Major Cousland and Colonel Capp rode back to West Point, chauffeured in an army sedan, mission accomplished.

———

In March, the 39-year-old writer arrived on the campus, located 50 miles north of New York on a promontory overlooking the Hudson River. The talk was held in the auditorium, and until Nelle took her seat on the stage, the 700 young men in gray uniforms remained standing. "After the introduction formalities, she began lighting a cigarette," said Capp, "but, turning to Major Cousland and referring to the cadet on her left, asked, 'Can he smoke?' 'No,' said Mike, 'he can't.' 'Then, I can't either,' she replied and stubbed out her cigarette in the nearest ashtray."[16]

The young men studied her. She was "conservatively garbed in a simple dark dress," according to former cadet Gus Lee, who later wrote *Honor and Duty* about his experiences at West Point, "her hair wrapped in a conservative bun atop her head. Her voice was softly Southern, with high musical notes, and crystal clear in a hall that was utterly silent."[17]

"This is very exciting," she began slowly, "because I do not speak at colleges. The prospect of it is too intimidating. Surely, it's obvious—rows of bright, intense, focused students, some even of the sciences, all of them analyzing my every word and staring fixedly at me—this would terrify a person such as myself. So I wisely agreed to come here, where the atmosphere would be far more relaxing and welcoming than on a rigid, strict, rule-bound, and severely disciplined college campus."

For the first time since becoming a class, the young men laughed together, and followed this with a roar of applause.

Knowing that the young men were away from home, she made a subtle comparison between aspects of *To Kill a Mockingbird* and the cadets' future mission as soldiers.

When we seek to replace family in new environs, we seek to reestablish trust, and love, and comfort. But too often we end up establishing difference instead of love. We like to have all our comforts and familiars about us, and tend to push away that which is different, and worrisome. That is what happened to Boo Radley, and to Tom Robinson. They were not set apart by evil men, or evil women, or evil thoughts. They were set apart by an evil past, which good people in the present were ill equipped to change. The irony is, if we divide ourselves for our own comfort, *no one* will have comfort. It means we must bury our pasts by seeing them, and destroy our differences through learning another way.

Regarding people who were difficult to accept or respect, Nelle said, "Our response to these people represents our earthly test. And I think, that these people enrich the wonder of our lives. It is they who most need our kindness, *because* they seem less deserving. After all, *anyone* can love people who are lovely."

She paused to reflect on how writing *To Kill a Mockingbird* had influenced her life. "People in the press have asked me if this book is descriptive of my own childhood, or of my own family. Is this very important? I am simply one who had time and chance to write. I was that person before, and no one in the press much cared about the details of my life. I am yet that same person now, who only misses her former anonymity."[18]

A few weeks after speaking at West Point, Nelle received another request for her presence, one that couldn't be further in spirit from speaking to an audience of hopeful, forward-looking young men. Perry Smith and Richard Hickock asked her to attend their execution. Nelle replied to Warden Charles McAtee, who had conveyed the request from Smith and Hickock, that she would not attend.

On the night of April 14, 1965, the executioner, an anonymous paid volunteer from Missouri, sped through the rain in a black Cadillac. He wore a long, dingy coat and large felt hat to hide his face. Smith, assuming both Nelle and Truman had denied his request, wrote a hasty note at 11:45 P.M.: "I want you to know that I cannot condemn you for it & understand. Not much time left but want you both to know that I been sincerely grateful for your friend[ship] through the years and everything else. I'm not very good at these things—I want you both to know that I have become very affectionate toward you. But harness time. Adios Amigos. Best of everything. Your friend always, Perry."[19]

In a hotel nearby, Truman agonized and wept in his room, trying to decide whether he should go or not. Hickock and Smith had the right to choose witnesses, and they had both named him and Nelle. Finally, Truman hurried to the prison in time to say good-bye. A handful of reporters and KBI agents were waiting in the warehouse. Hickock arrived first, trussed in a leather harness that held his arms to his sides. "Nice to see you," he said pleasantly, smiling at faces he recognized. He was pronounced dead at 12:41 A.M. When it was Perry's turn on the gallows, 20 minutes later, Capote became sick to his stomach.

———

For the rest of the summer of 1965 in Monroeville, Nelle buckled down to work. It had been five years since the publication of

To Kill a Mockingbird. She had been trading on her first novel for quite some time, although novelists often go years between books. But now she shunned interviews; first, because questions about *To Kill a Mockingbird* had become redundant. Second, because she had gone on record a number of times that a second novel was in the offing. So far, it was a promise she hadn't made good on. What she needed was "paper, pen, and privacy," the formula that had produced her first success.

She made one exception to turning down interviews, however. A young Mississippian, Don Keith, approached her about granting one for a small quarterly, the *Delta Review*. She consented to a "visit," not an interview, perhaps because she saw in the earnest young writer a glimpse of herself from her *Rammer Jammer* days.

Keith, who would go on to become a first-rate journalist in New Orleans, provided a remarkably fresh portrait of Lee, placing her in the context of a writer at work. "When I met her that Sunday afternoon in Monroeville, Alabama, she was the same as I knew she would be. We had spoken twice briefly over the telephone. I had written her two letters; she had written me one. But regardless of the long distance acquaintance, we exchanged hello kisses in that familiar manner characteristic of Southerners. Once inside the modest but comfortable brick house," they settled down to a "long talk over coffee and cigarettes. She consumes both in abundance."[20]

The young visitor was the first to use the term *recluse* in connection with Nelle, but he did so for the sake of denying she was one. "Harper Lee is no recluse," he said. "She is real and down-to-earth as is the woman next door who puts up fig preserves in the spring and covers her chrysanthemums in winter.

"During most of our afternoon together, she sat at a card table placed in front of an armchair in the living room. On the table was a typewriter, not new, and an abundance of paper. A stack of finished manuscript lay nearby, work on a new novel." Nelle explained that she hadn't set a deadline for it, and that her publisher, Lippincott, didn't know the entire plot yet. But she hinted that it was set in a Southern town again, perhaps Maycomb. Whether Jem, Scout, and Atticus would figure in the story, she wouldn't say.

The conversation turned to another literary project that needed her attention. She was scheduled to leave the next week for New York, where she was to read, before publication, Truman Capote's finished manuscript.

"It must seem a chore," Keith said.

"But one I'm looking forward to," replied Nelle. As always, she was Truman's friend and advocate.

———

Besides needing to be in New York to read Truman's typewritten manuscript of *In Cold Blood*, it was time for her doctor to examine her injured hand and see whether surgery would be required. Everyone hoped for a good prognosis. "We were all looking at her hand and were pleased and surprised how beautifully it has healed. We hope when she sees Dr. Stark on the 19th [of September] that he will tell her she doesn't have to have the operation," Annie Laurie wrote to Alice.[21]

Nelle could hold a pen or pencil again, but her fingers'

movement was slightly constricted and her handwriting, normally open and highly legible, looked compressed. Perhaps because of this, she jotted succinct comments on Truman's pages. Regarding a piece of dialogue, for instance, she noted, "Everybody talks in short sentences. Mannered."

In August, *McCall's* magazine published "When Children Discover America," her first piece since *Vogue* carried "Love— In Other Words" in 1961. But the new article, just like the *Vogue* essay, showed none of her hallmark humor or vividness. In fact, a strong whiff of self-righteousness replaced the exuberance that readers would have expected from the author of *To Kill a Mockingbird*. It was as if her high spirits and wit were being tamped down by too much self-consciousness now, perhaps a result of being in the public eye.

> I don't think, for instance, that the Lincoln Memorial needs to be pointed out to any human being of any age. I would let children discover the beauty and mystery and grandeur of it. They'll ask questions later. No child can possibly leave the Lincoln Memorial without questions, often important questions. . . . Younger children may not respond in words, but they will drink everything in with their eyes, and fill their minds with awareness and wonder. It's an experience they will enjoy and remember all their lives; and it will give them greater pride in their own country.[22]

Truman, meanwhile, was certain he was on the verge of volcanic fame, and he was feeling ecstatic about it. *The New Yorker* would begin serializing *In Cold Blood* in four consecutive issues. On September 25, 1965, the first installment appeared, beginning with the oft-quoted sentence "The village of Holcomb stands on the high wheat plains of western Kansas, a lonesome area that other Kansans call 'out there.'"

The New Yorker's circulation went through the roof, and sightseers poured down the elm-lined road to the Clutters' old house.[23]

———

Nelle's physician decided that an operation would be necessary after all, otherwise scar tissue would permanently impair her hand. Maurice and Annie Laurie arranged to take her to the hospital, see that she was comfortable, and be there for her when she awoke from the anesthetic.

The operation was a success. "We are so thrilled that Nelle had such a good report from Dr. Stark yesterday," Annie Laurie wrote to Alice. "She sounds like a different person on the phone because now she knows her hand is going to be all right. She will be able to use it for writing and playing golf."[24]

The timing was perfect, because Nelle's high school English teacher, Gladys Watson-Burkett, was coming to New York at Nelle's invitation. The teacher and former student were about to embark, on October 8, on a memorable month-long trip to England, and Nelle had insisted on paying for the excursion. "It was a thank-you for editing her manuscript," said Sarah Countryman, Gladys's daughter.[25]

But a completed second novel had not materialized before Nelle left on vacation, and Tay Hohoff was getting tired of the delay. Anne Laurie sprang to Nelle's defense. "I told [Nelle] that I thought it was better the way things turned out about her second book, as she was under pressure and thought she had to write it this summer," she assured Alice.

> It doesn't have to be written according [to] her publisher's schedule and I think she should take her time and not try to work on the book until she gets back down to Alabama with her folks. . . . Too many people up here ask too many questions and she seems to feel that she is expected to turn in another manuscript, because everybody says, "Are you working on another novel.[?]" I always say "Of course, she is going to write another book but she is not *going to be hurried.*" It is difficult, as you know to follow Mockingbird as this book was such an all-around success that measuring up to that book is almost impossible. *But she is a writer* and her next book will be a success too, and will have some of the flavor of the first one.[26]

Nelle returned from England in November. She knew, as everyone did, that *In Cold Blood* would be out soon in hardback. The magazine serialization in *The New Yorker* had served as a drumroll leading up to the book's publication. For Nelle, it would be the end to a long experience. More than five years earlier, she had supported Truman in Garden City when he felt discouraged. Then, for two months, she had served as his listening post in town and made friends with the folks he needed to interview. Later, she had accompanied him on return trips: once to attend the trial, and two more times just to go over the territory, sifting, sifting for more information. "Without her

deep probing of the people of that little town," Truman told
Alabama author Wayne Greenhaw, "I could never have done
the job I did with it."[27] And finally, she had tightened up his
manuscript while she was supposed to be working on her second novel.

So when, in January 1966, she opened the first edition of *In
Cold Blood*, she was shocked. The book was dedicated, first, to
Capote's longtime lover, Jack Dunphy, and, second, to her.
There was no hint of how much she had helped.

Nelle was not a woman who was quick to anger or demanding of attention. But "Nelle was very hurt that she didn't get
more credit because she wrote half that book. Harper was
really pissed about that. She told me several times," recalled
R. Philip Hanes, who became friends with her later that year.[28]
She was "written out of that book at the last minute," main-
tained Claudia Durst Johnson, a scholar who has published
extensively about *To Kill a Mockingbird*. Not even the short
acknowledgment page, which mentioned other people, paid
tribute to Nelle's large and important contribution.[29]

Truman's failure to appreciate her was more than an over-
sight or a letdown. It was a betrayal. Since childhood, he had
been testing her friendship, because perhaps, deep down, he
believed that no one, including her, really liked him—not since
his parents had withdrawn their love. He was constantly showing off to get people's attention and approval, all while gauging
their response. But hurting her so unnecessarily, perhaps to see
what she would do, spoke volumes about whether she could
trust him. She would remain his friend, but their relationship
had suffered its first permanent crack.

Truman Capote in front of the Clutter home after In Cold Blood *became a sensation. He downplayed Nelle's role in creating the book. (Corbis)*

If Truman suspected the amount of damage he had done to their lifelong friendship, he doesn't seem to have taken special steps to repair it. For instance, he could have counteracted rumors that he had written all or part of *To Kill a Mockingbird*, but he never went to any strenuous lengths to deny it.[30]

———

On November 28, 1966, all of New York society was agog with Truman's "Black and White Ball," held at the Plaza Hotel. It was, Truman told the press, a "little masked ball for Kay Graham [president of the *Washington Post* and *Newsweek* magazine] and all my friends." It was also to celebrate the success of *In Cold Blood*, but Truman wasn't saying that.

Five hundred and forty of his friends had received invitations, but red and white admission tickets were printed only the week before to prevent forgeries. Stairways and elevators were blocked, except for one elevator going up to the ballroom. From its doors emerged the glitterati of the times: politicians, scientists, painters, writers, composers, actors, producers, dress designers, social figures, and tycoons, including Frank Sinatra; William F. Buckley; poet Marianne Moore; Countess Agnelli, wife of Henry Ford II; Mr. and Mrs. Norman Mailer; and Rose Kennedy. Truman invited ten guests from Kansas, too, including Alvin and Marie Dewey and the widow of Judge Roland Tate. Secret Service agents made a mental note of everyone getting off the elevator, and the guests were announced as they entered the ballroom.

Nelle received an invitation, but she didn't attend, an indication of how much she wanted to distance herself from *In Cold Blood* and everything associated with it.

———

By the 1970s, Nelle's surrogate family, the community that had sustained her through the creation of her first novel and whom she had relied upon for guidance when she was a beginning writer, had grown smaller. She saw Michael and Joy Brown regularly whenever she was in New York, but their friendship continued regardless of whether Nelle wrote or not. Maurice had died in April 1970 of cancer, and Annie Laurie had closed their agency. Truman's place in Nelle's life was uncertain because he was drinking and using drugs heavily, a result of strain caused by *In Cold Blood*, he said. She was prepared to stand by him, but he was difficult, even to people who genuinely cared about him.

Getting a manuscript to Tay Hohoff no longer mattered, either, because Tay had retired from Lippincott. Besides, the excitement about another novel from Nelle Harper Lee had long worn off. It had been more than ten years since *To Kill a Mockingbird.*

Then, in 1974, Tay Hohoff, widowed since the death of her husband, Arthur, some years before, died in her apartment the night before she was to move in with in-laws.

"I think it's fair to say that Nelle owes her immediate success to her relationship with Tay," said Alabama writer Wayne Greenhaw. "They were very close and it just devastated Nelle when she died."[31]

About the same time, a film producer visiting Monroeville for a BBC documentary asked Alice whatever happened to the second novel her sister was supposed to be working on. According to Alice, just as Nelle was finishing it, a burglar broke into her apartment and stole the manuscript.[32]

And that excuse, as unbelievable as it sounds, was the last ever said by the Lee family about a second novel from Harper Lee.

Chapter 10

Quiet Time

Gʟɪᴍᴘsᴇs ᴏꜰ Hᴀʀᴘᴇʀ Lᴇᴇ ᴅᴜʀɪɴɢ ᴍᴏsᴛ ᴏꜰ ᴛʜᴇ 1970s and '80s were as infrequent as spotting a rare bird, native to the South, in New York's Central Park. Since 1967 she had been living in a small apartment, only her third address since arriving in the city almost 20 years earlier. All of the apartments where she had lived were within a 15-minute walk of one another, and none was particularly luxurious. She wasn't living like a rich person; that wasn't her style. The new place, a four-story brick building, would have looked quite ordinary to most passersby. "I couldn't pick it out from a hundred others," said a visiting friend.[1]

It seemed the perfect camouflage for someone who wanted to go unnoticed. Lining her side of the street were a dozen stunted trees. The usual collection of commercial property interrupted the eye's sweep of the block. There was a dry cleaner's, a travel agent, and a restaurant serving wild game. The only hint of community was a storefront church.

Inside her apartment, the décor was unexceptional, too.

There were no indications that she was the author of a book that had sold nearly 10 million copies by the late 1970s. A visitor couldn't recall anything special about it years later.

Slowly, her world was becoming smaller. Although she continued a pattern of returning to Monroeville every October and staying until spring, she remained close to familiar haunts while in New York. "I honestly, *truly* have not the slightest idea *why* she lives in New York," said Truman in an interview. "I don't think she ever goes *out*."[2] When a friend visiting from Alabama suggested they meet near Rockefeller Center for dinner, Nelle objected. "My God, I wouldn't go into downtown Manhattan for the world!"[3] Any new venture seemed to make her hesitate. Horton Foote marveled that Nelle lived within blocks of mutual friends of theirs for years without ever contacting them.

Instead, she preferred friends from long ago. She corresponded regularly with Ralph Hammond, a writer from her days on the *Rammer Jammer* at the University of Alabama. ("I've got a whole drawerful of letters from Nelle," he liked to boast, "she's my best friend in all of Alabama.")[4] And Joy Brown could always be relied on for shopping trips and jaunts to secondhand bookstores.

Nelle's oldest friend, however, Truman, whose ties with her spanned Monroeville and New York, seemed to be undergoing a slow-motion breakdown she was unable to stop. Fears and regrets assailed him. When *People* magazine requested an interview in 1976, he brought Nelle along for comfort. As he was describing his unhappy childhood, she interjected that the kindergarten teacher in Monroeville had smacked his palm with a ruler because he knew how to read.

"It's true!" Truman wailed.

Glancing protectively at him, Nelle explained, "It was traumatic."[5]

Truman's deterioration became newsworthy in July 1978 when he appeared as a guest on *The Stanley Siegel Show* radio program in New York. During the first few minutes, he seemed all right, but gradually his speech became slurred and hesitant. Clearly, there were problems.

"What's going to happen unless you lick this problem of drugs and alcohol?" Siegel asked.

Seconds of dead air followed while Truman tried to rally himself. Finally, he replied in a croaky voice, "The obvious answer is that eventually I'll kill myself."[6]

He hung on for several more years, washing up now and then like driftwood in hospital emergency rooms, until he died in 1984, a few weeks short of his sixtieth birthday. His last words were for his mother, Lillie Mae, who had committed suicide years before.

Nelle, along with Al and Marie Dewey, attended Truman's memorial service in Los Angeles, where the first chapter of *In Cold Blood* was read aloud as a tribute. Afterward, they went to the home of one of Truman's friends from happier times, novelist Donald Windham. When Windham asked Nelle during dinner when the last time was she'd spoken to Truman, she had to say she hadn't heard from him in a very long while.

Truman's death ended a long chapter in Nelle's life. But it also spun her thoughts back 25 years to those Kansas days when she'd been most creative. In 1960, she had been his "assistant researchist," contributing to one of the most sensational and highly regarded books in American literature, while her first novel, *To Kill a Mockingbird*, was just months away from publication. That brief period had been the highest point of her writing life thus far.

And so, in the mid-1980s, retracing her steps over familiar ground, Nelle embarked on a book project that resembled *In Cold Blood*. It would be a "nonfiction novel" based on a serial murder case in Alabama she'd read about involving a man accused of killing relatives for their insurance money. And this time, unlike *In Cold Blood*, the book and the credit would belong wholly to her. The working title she chose was *The Reverend*.[7]

The story revolves around W. M. "Willie Jo" Maxwell, a veteran of World War II, born and raised in east Alabama. During the mid-1970s, in addition to working in the wood pulp business, he did some preaching on the side in black churches in Alexander City and became known as the Reverend Maxwell. One night, Tom Radney, Sr., an attorney and former state senator, received a call from Maxwell. "You've got to come out here to my home," Maxwell pleaded, "the police are saying I killed my wife." Mrs. Maxwell had been found tied to a tree about a mile outside of town and murdered.

Radney agreed to take the case. Fortunately for the reverend, the woman next door provided him with an alibi and he was found not guilty. From a portion of his late wife's insurance policy, Maxwell paid Radney's fees. Later, he married the woman next door.

"A year or so passed," said Radney, "and then the new wife showed up dead."

Again Maxwell asked Radney to defend him. During the

trial, the jury was persuaded that there was no evidence linking Maxwell to the murder. He was acquitted, and he paid Radney from his second wife's insurance policy.

The third time Maxwell was charged with murder was in connection with his brother, who was found dead by the side of a road. The district attorney argued that Reverend Maxwell, either by himself or with someone's help, had poured liquor down his brother's throat until he died of alcohol poisoning. But the jury wasn't convinced and returned another verdict of not guilty. Maxwell was his brother's beneficiary and had another lump sum due him. The Alexander City Police Department began referring to Radney's law offices as the "Maxwell Building."

The fourth death involved Maxwell's nephew, discovered dead behind the wheel of his car. Apparently, he had run into a tree. The following day, Radney, retained again as Maxwell's attorney, inspected the crash site. "Not even the largest trees were more than two inches around," he said. "It was obvious that hitting those little trees didn't kill the reverend's nephew. However, the state could not prove the cause of death. I remember having a pathologist on the witness stand. I asked him, 'C'mon, what did he die of?' And the reply was, 'Judge, I hate to tell you, but we don't know what he died of.'" Maxwell left the courtroom a free man and settled with Radney from proceeds from his nephew's insurance policy.

The fifth death touching the reverend appeared on the front page of the *Alexander City Outlook* on June 15, 1977. Police reported that Shirley Ellington, Maxwell's teenage niece, had been changing a flat tire when her car fell off the jack and killed her. After reading the news story, Radney decided, "I've had enough." When Maxwell showed up at his offices, his erstwhile attorney turned him down.

"Mr. Radney, you're not being fair to me," Maxwell protested. "I have done nothing wrong. You've got to defend me."

Radney later recalled the next few minutes clearly. "I said, 'Reverend, enough's enough. Maybe you're innocent, you never told me anything differently, and I'll never say a word against you, but I will not defend you anymore.' In the meantime, the area behind my office building was filled with cameras and reporters from Birmingham, Montgomery, and Columbus, Georgia. A newswoman was standing behind his car, and the last thing I heard the reverend say as he got into his big Chrysler was, 'Ma'am, if you don't move, I'm going to run over you.'"

The police waited to arrest him, hoping Maxwell might do or say something during his niece's funeral service that would incriminate him. Instead, a scene took place that Nelle decided was the perfect beginning to *The Reverend*, one that was both awful and comic in one stroke.

A week after Shirley Ellington's death from being crushed underneath a car, 300 people gathered for her memorial service in the chapel of the House of Hutcheson funeral home. One of the teenager's uncles, Robert Burns from Chicago, took a seat in the pew behind Maxwell. As the organist was playing and the choir singing in the loft, Burns took out a .45 from his suit jacket and shot Maxwell point-blank in the back. For a moment, Maxwell dabbed at his forehead with a handkerchief while blood spilled from his mouth. Then he fell to the floor, dead. All the mourners ran for the doors, but finding police blocking the exits, they pushed back inside.

"Two or three ladies, little heavy ones," said Radney, "tried to get out the windows and got stuck. The preacher didn't stop preaching, he just got under the pulpit. The organist got under the organ and kept playing, and the choir in the choir loft kept singing—nothing stopped. The next day, police found more than a dozen guns and twice as many knives scattered under the pews."

That's where Nelle would end her first chapter.[8]

Radney defended Burns, after first checking with the Alabama Bar Association that it wouldn't be a conflict of interest. But since Maxwell was dead, there was none. The jury was out 20 minutes and came back with a verdict of not guilty. The judge sent Burns on his way. As court adjourned, the district attorney mused aloud that he must be the only prosecutor in the United States to have lost a first-degree murder case when there were 300 witnesses.

The Maxwell killings were tailor-made for someone with Nelle's experience. Moreover, Radney said he was "really excited about the possibility of a book or movie" when she contacted him about giving the story an *In Cold Blood* treatment. He agreed to share all his files going back to the beginning, when he first met the reverend. For the movie version, she said she wanted him to play the defense counsel. Gregory Peck would probably get the lead. (Peck, who had kept up his friendship over the years, was bewildered when she said she had a really good part for him if he could play an old woman! "I'm not sure she was kidding," he mused.)[9]

For about a year she made her writing headquarters the Horseshoe Bend Motel in Alexander City where she pored over the records of the trials and took notes on the setting. Then she shifted to her sister Louise's house in Eufaula for three months. Louise, though never especially interested in her sister's writing, was glad for company because her husband, Herschel, was in poor health. During the next few years, Nelle would call Radney with updates on how the book was progressing, sometimes saying that it was practically done. "The galleys are at the publishers; it should be published in about a week," she would say. But nothing materialized.

Impatient with being put off about the book any longer, Radney went to New York to retrieve his files. After that, he gradually stopped hearing from Nelle. "Don't bring up writing," a friend of hers cautioned William Smart, a college professor whose creative writing classes Nelle had addressed years earlier. "She's very sensitive about that."[10]

Nelle's conflicted feelings about writing, the past, and the invasiveness of publicity came to a head in 1988 with the publication of Gerald Clarke's bestselling *Capote: A Biography*. Reminiscing to Clarke, a former reporter for *Time* magazine, about growing up next door to the Lees, Truman told tales about the family and Mrs. Lee's emotional problems. "When they talk about Southern grotesque, they're not kidding!"[11]

Nelle was outraged. There was no more vulnerable and painful side of her life he could have touched on. "I hope you read the book with a salt-shaker at your side," she wrote to

Caldwell Delaney, an old friend and former director of the Museum of Mobile.[12]

> Truman's vicious lie—that my mother was mentally unbal-anced and tried twice to kill me (that gentle soul's reward for having loved him)—was the first example of his legacy to his friends. Truman left, in the book, something hateful and untrue about every one of them, which more than anything should tell you what was plain to us for more than the last fif-teen years of his life—he was paranoid to a terrifying degree. Drugs and alcohol did not cause his insanity, they were the result of it.
>
> If you found yourself in a Monroeville that was strange to you, remember that Gerald Clarke was on his own for the first time, without the fact-checking services of TIME, Inc., and relied on information from Truman's relatives!

Protecting her legacy became important to Nelle, as the chances of her publishing again seemed more and more unlikely. At one point, her cousin Dickie Williams asked her, "When are you going to come out with another book?" And she said, "Rich-ard, when you're at the top there's only one way to go."[13] She meant *down* in readers' esteem.

Meanwhile, her hometown, Monroeville, had realized its singular advantage as the birthplace of the author who had written one of the most popular and truly influential novels of the 20th century. By 1988, the National Council of Teachers of English reported that *To Kill a Mockingbird* was taught in 74 percent of the nation's public schools. Only *Romeo and Juliet*, *Macbeth*, and *Huckleberry Finn* were assigned more often. In addition, Monroeville enjoyed a second distinction as the setting for the novel, which no other town could claim.

So in 1990, the 30th anniversary of the publication of *To Kill a Mockingbird*, Monroeville staged its first production of the play based on the novel, adapted and licensed for amateur theatrical use by Christopher Sergel, owner of Dramatic Publishing. As far back as 1965, Sergel had persuaded Annie Laurie that "Schools all across the country continue to write to us with requests for a dramatization of *To Kill a Mockingbird*—it is much more requested than *any* other book."[14] Thus Monroeville was tardy in embracing its literary heritage by 25 years, but eager to see what the local response would be.

The Monroeville staging of *To Kill a Mockingbird* had charms that no other production could match. Audience members sat in chairs and risers placed outside the courthouse, next to sidewalks where Nelle roller-skated as a child. Huge pecan trees provided a natural canopy above the sets representing porches on the street where the Finches live. The cast, consisting of residents—businesspeople, farmers, students—rehearsed for weeks in the evenings, trying to recapture the Depression in Alabama, though few could personally recall it. Some hoped that Nelle might make an encouraging appearance at their inaugural opening night, but they were destined to be disappointed. "She sorts of hates publicity," said Nelle's agent at McIntosh and Otis, an understatement for those who were unfamiliar with Nelle's ways by 1990. "The book stands. Which in a way is wonderful."[15]

The first act unfolded under trees by the side of the court-house, where mockingbirds can be heard singing in the branches. When Atticus raised a rifle to shoot an imaginary mad dog in the distance, the children in the audience gleefully covered their ears. *Bang*! echoed off the storefronts on the square. For the scene when Atticus defies a lynch mob bent on kidnapping his client, the courthouse's side door doubled as the entrance to the jailhouse. Across the street was the actual jail Nelle had in mind.

During intermission, the actor playing the sheriff called the names of 12 white males in the audience for jury duty—the only citizens eligible to serve under the laws of Alabama in the 1930s. Coolers heaped with ice offered drinks and snacks dur-ing the break to combat the weather that, as early as May, is already muggy.

Once inside the courthouse for the start of the second act, the audience settled into the pewlike benches. Up in the "colored" gallery, members of a local black church sat and watched, a poignant reminder of how things once were. In the jury box, a dozen white men prepared to hear the case.

Everyone knew the trial's outcome, although in the stuffy courtroom built in 1903, with one ceiling fan turning tiredly high above, there was a sense that the sins of history could be reversed if only the jury would find Tom Robinson not guilty. When the foreman led the jury back into the court-room, Robinson was again convicted for a crime he hadn't committed.

The play was such a success—both in attendance and for the boost it gave civic pride—that the following year, 1991, the

Monroe County Heritage Museums hired a director to capital-
ize further on Monroeville's link with *To Kill a Mockingbird*. In
light of such a tribute to the novel and its creator, few could
have anticipated that it would be the start of an uneasy
relationship between Nelle and the town.

———

As the annual performances of *To Kill a Mockingbird* in Monroeville became more popular, and the Monroe County Heritage Museums tended to put more emphasis on Monroeville's
link to Harper Lee, the author was not pleased to see that her
birthplace was getting on the *Mockingbird* bandwagon, so to
speak. For her, this meant more requests for autographs, more
fan mail, and more occasions when strangers would quiz her
about the book. At a Christmas party one year in Monroeville,
an out-of-towner began chatting her up about *To Kill a Mockingbird*. She turned and walked out.[16]

By now Nelle was in her 70s and weary of the attention
connected with her novel. She had put that far behind her, along
with the film. She rebuffed attempts by Mary Badham, the child
actor who played Scout, to communicate with her. "Mary acts
like that book is the Bible," Nelle mentioned to Kathy McCoy,
the former director of the Monroe County Heritage Museums.[17] According to a terse note in the museums' archives,
"G.P. [Gregory Peck] told M.B. not to try to contact N.L." Not
even invitations to receive honors could induce Nelle to depart
from her well-worn path. Twice, Huntingdon College in the
1990s asked her to attend graduation. She never replied.[18] The
University of Alabama succeeded in awarding her an honorary

degree in 1993 (perhaps the appeal for Nelle was closure after never having graduated), but all she would say to the audience was "Thank you."

The distance she felt from her only novel was unmistakable in a foreword to the 35th anniversary edition in 1993. "Please spare *Mockingbird* an Introduction," she wrote.

> As a reader I loathe Introductions. To novels, I associate Introductions with long-gone authors and works that are being brought back into print after decades of internment. Although *Mockingbird* will be 35 this year, it has never been out of print and I am still alive, although very quiet. Introductions inhibit pleasure, they kill the joy of anticipation, they frustrate curiosity. The only good thing about Introductions is that in some cases they delay the dose to come. *Mockingbird* still says what it has to say; it has managed to survive without preamble.

With dismay, she watched the transformation of Monroeville into the "Literary Capital of Alabama." After volunteers had finished painting 12-foot-high outdoor murals of scenes from the novel, Nelle pronounced them "graffiti." When a television crew asked to film portions of the play and interview the actors, she responded through her agent, "Not just no, but *hell* no."[19]

According to Reverend Thomas Butts, one of her closest friends and the retired minister for Monroeville's First Methodist Church, "She isn't too happy about any of it." Apparently her friend and counselor was referring to the rise of *Mockingbird* tourism in Monroeville, which as of 2005 brings in about 25,000 visitors annually. Said Reverend Butts, her attitude is a combination of wanting privacy and resenting people looking to profit, without permission, from her or her book.

"She would give you the shirt off her back," added the reverend's wife, "but do not try to take it without permission."[20]

Going ahead without permission caused the most serious showdown between Nelle and the Monroe County Heritage Museums. It was over a cookbook.

Calpurnia's Cookbook, named for the Finches' cook and housekeeper, was the typical kind of recipe collection assembled by churches to raise money. Only, in this case, the idea was that profits from the sale would support the museums. When Nelle got wind that one of her characters' names would soon be appearing beside *To Kill a Mockingbird* pens, coffee mugs, and T-shirts in the courthouse museum gift shop, she threatened to sue. The entire printing of the cookbook, several thousand copies, had to be pulped.

"I think it is an attempt to keep the characters from being exploited, as well as herself," Reverend Butts said. "When people start using the characters from the book, it sort of fragments the book. They're using it to promote their hamburgers or their automobiles or their own [things]. She wants the characters from *To Kill a Mockingbird* to stay back in the '30s where they belong. To drag them by the hair on their head into the 21st Century is to do the characters an injustice."[21]

In the town's defense, the late-20th century hadn't been kind to Monroeville. The only major industry, Vanity Fair, a lingerie factory, shut down some years ago, laying off hundreds of workers and pulling the plug on one of Monroe County's main sources of tax revenue. Today, in many ways, Monroeville fits Nelle's description of its alter ego, Maycomb, in the 1930s. It's "a tired old town," except for the money spent by tourists on meals, gas, trinkets in the museum gift shop, and tickets to the annual play. Monroeville's hope for a better day partly depends on promoting its most famous resident, Harper Lee— the "golden goose," some residents call her.[22]

———

Yet Nelle's secluded life and decades-long anonymity continue to exert a fascination for newspaper editors and other media people looking for a good story. Feature stories headlined "What Ever Happened to Harper Lee?" crop up several times a year. As Reverend Butts rightly observed, "Whether she intended to or not, she created a mystique when she withdrew from the public eye like that."[23]

Mostly the reporters who visit Monroeville get a feel for the town and interview a handful of people who knew Nelle. Phone interviews with her are impossible because Alice, still in the role of her sister's manager, politely turns down requests.

On the other hand, some encounters with Nelle have been memorable when pilgrims to Monroeville have behaved with a modicum of respect. Reporter Kathy Kemp took a chance one evening in 1997 and rang the doorbell of the Lees' home.[24] Nelle opened the door.

> She was not expecting company. Barefoot, white hair uncombed, the 71-year-old woman answered the doorbell wearing a long white pajama top and a scowl.
>
> "What is it?" Harper Lee wanted to know.

Staring at her through the storm door were a reporter and a photographer from Birmingham. Miss Lee has a famous dislike for reporters and photographers. We'd been warned, repeatedly, by folks all over town, "Don't even think of trying to do an interview."

Instead, we thrust forth a copy of "To Kill A Mockingbird" and asked for her autograph.

"Good gosh," Miss Lee exclaimed, a look of disgust on her face. "It's a little late for this sort of thing, isn't it?"

It wasn't yet 6 P.M. on a balmy Tuesday. Folks on her street in the small southwestern Alabama town of Monroeville were just coming home from work. Televisions blared through open windows. Schoolchildren played in front yards.

We apologized.

"Just a minute then," she snapped before disappearing into the house. Seconds later, she was back with her fine-point pen and an even more pointed lecture. "I hope you're more polite to other people," she said as she opened the book to the title page.

"Best wishes, Harper Lee," she wrote in a neat, modest script.

She handed back the volume. "Next time try to be more thoughtful."

"Thank you," we said, frankly terrified. And for the first time since opening the door, Harper Lee smiled. In a voice full of warmth and good cheer, she replied, "You're quite welcome."

The best kind of interaction tends to occur when Nelle is free to be spontaneous. Then her warmth and generosity, known mainly to close friends and family, become evident.

Nelle applauds as the winner of a To Kill a Mockingbird *high school essay contest is announced on January 23, 2004, in Tuscaloosa, Alabama. (AP Photo)*

At the May 2006 University of Notre Dame commencement, Nelle received an honorary degree. Students held up copies of To Kill a Mockingbird *provided by the university. (AP Photo)*

"One day many years ago when she was signing books at The Magnolia Cottage, a specialty shop in Monroeville," said Mary Tomlinson,

I was walking in as she was walking out. I told her who I was and that I played volleyball with her at Huntingdon. I told her my name, knowing that she would probably not remember this fledgling freshman. I told her I hoped I could get an autographed copy of her book for my granddaughter. She smiled, patted my hand and said, "Mary, I'm sorry, I actually do not remember you." Then she added, "But I'll be happy to sign your granddaughter's book." She waited until I could go inside and purchase it for her signature and a short note. She couldn't have been more tactful or genuine.[25]

And she evinces a special affection for young readers, sometimes responding positively to requests to visit local high schools for book-signings or unpublicized appearances. "I was in the National Honor Society at Monroe County High School," said student Amanda McMillan,

and every year we induct an honorary member at our induction ceremony. My sophomore year it was Alice, Harper Lee's sister, because she's the oldest practicing female attorney in Alabama.

[The adviser] didn't tell us because they didn't think she would say yes. But since she went to high school there, she thought it was super-cool and agreed to it. Our president was there, but he had a leg cast, so I had to hand her the plaque. I was sitting next to Miss Alice, and Harper Lee was on the other side of her.

I heard her talking to Miss Alice (who is partially deaf, so she was talking pretty loudly), and she said, "I don't get nervous at these things anymore. You want to know why?" Miss Alice asked why, and Harper Lee said, "'Cause you and I are the oldest ones here!"[26]

According to Don Collins, a former Methodist minister in Alabama, Nelle has funded scholarships over the years. "Many have attended college without knowing she was their benefactor."[27]

———

In 2006, Nelle turned 80; Alice was 95. They both wear hearing aids that go *Wheeee!* in diners at times and then they argue about whose is making noise. They often debate whose turn it is to get the check, too, a discussion that usually ends with "I'll get it this time, and you next time." Nelle dotes on her older sister, whom she calls "Atticus in a skirt" because of Alice's achievements in law, particularly with regard to integrating the Methodist Church over the years.

For Alice's birthday a few years ago, some friends pulled up to the Lees' home early in the morning. The two sisters followed in their Buick, with Nelle at the wheel, until they reached Vanity Fair Park. Robert Sims, the city superintendent, was there waiting. While Nelle and Alice watched, two workers lifted a large box from the bed of a pickup truck and opened it. Out waddled two large geese, who headed for the edge of the pond a few yards away. From a second small box issued three baby mallards. The ducklings were gently steered into a safe, penned-in area in shallow water. The event, which brought children on the run to see what was going on, was part of the park's effort to replenish the supply of waterfowl, which hawks and foxes had decimated. Alice was charmed by it all. "These new park residents should continue to bring pleasure to people from 92 down," she wrote to family gaily.[28]

While in Monroeville, Nelle spends most of her time at home reading. Inside the entryway of the Lees' one-story brick ranch are photographs of family members. But everywhere else are books: in a bookcase that takes up half the entrance hallway; in Alice's bedroom, off the kitchen; and in Nelle's blue bedroom, at the end of the hallway. In her room, the walls are devoted to built-in white bookshelves, floor to ceiling. A third bedroom, for guests, has bookshelves, too. As in Nelle's apartment in New York, there are no expensive furnishings that would indicate she is the author of the bestselling novel of the 20th century. On the contrary, the Lees' home is unremarkable in every way.

"Those things have no meaning for Nelle Harper," Alice said. "All she needs is a good bed, a bathroom and a type-writer. . . . Books are the things she cares about."[29]

In 60 years, Nelle has never attended a reunion of the sisters of the Chi Omega house at the University of Alabama. "I've written to her many times," said a Chi O member, "and she's never acknowledged receipt of my letter."[30] But a street on campus is named Harper Lee Drive.

An anecdote floating around on the Internet in 2005 said

that a waiter at a party in New York recognized Harper Lee sitting by herself at a table. Unable to resist the temptation to express his admiration, he struck up a friendly conversation with her and asked the inevitable, "Why didn't you write another book?"[31]

She reportedly had every intention of writing many novels, but never could have imagined the success *To Kill a Mockingbird* would enjoy. She became overwhelmed. Every waking hour seemed devoted to the promotion and publicity surrounding the book. Time passed, she said, and she retreated from the spotlight. She claimed to be inherently shy and was never comfortable with too much attention. Fame had never meant anything to her, and she was not prepared for what *To Kill a Mockingbird* achieved.

Then before she knew it, nearly a decade had passed and she was nowhere near finishing a new book. Rather than allow herself to be eternally frustrated, she simply "forgave herself" and lifted the burden from her shoulders of living up to her first book. And she refused to pressure herself into writing another novel unless the muse came to her naturally.

A little more than a year after *To Kill a Mockingbird* was published, Nelle wrote to a friend in Mobile, "People who have made peace with themselves are the people I most admire in the world."[32]

From all indications, she seems to have done that.

Notes

Page numbers are given wherever possible.

Chapter 1: "Ellen" Spelled Backward

1. George Thomas Jones, "Young Harper Lee's Affinity for Fighting," letter to EducETH "Teaching and Learning," http://educeth.ethz.ch/, 7 December 1999, accessed 17 January 2002.
2. Freda Roberson Noble, letter to author, 18 September 2002.
3. Truman Capote, "The Thanksgiving Visitor," in *A Christmas Memory, One Christmas, & The Thanksgiving Visitor* (New York: Modern Library, 1996).
4. Drew Jubera, "To Find a Mockingbird," *Dallas Times Herald*, 1984.
5. Freda Roberson Noble, letter to author, 18 September 2002.
6. "'Luckiest Person in the World,' Says Pulitzer Winner," *Birmingham News*, 2 May 1961.
7. *National Archives and Records Service*, College Park, Md., 15th Alabama Infantry files. Harper Lee's family can be traced back to John Lee, Esq., born in 1695 in Nansemond, Virginia, but her family and General Lee's are separate.
8. A. C. Lee, *Monroe Journal* (editorial), 19 December 1929, 2.
9. Harper Lee, *To Kill a Mockingbird* (New York: Warner Books, 1982), 4.
10. *Ninth Annual Catalogue of the Alabama Girls' Industrial School*, Montevallo, Alabama, 1904–1905 (Montgomery, Ala.: Brown Printing Co.), 20.
11. Ibid., 38.
12. Kathy Painter McCoy, *Letters from the Civil War: Monroe County Remembers Her Rebel Sons* (Monroeville, Ala.: Monroe County Heritage Museums, 1992).
13. "Old Monroe County Courthouse," (flyer, no date) Monroe County Heritage Museums.

14. Lee, *To Kill a Mockingbird*, 131.

15. Marie Faulk Rudisill, with James C. Simmons. *Truman Capote: The Story of His Bizarre and Exotic Childhood by an Aunt Who Helped Raise Him* (New York: William Morrow, 1983), 190.

16. Jubera, "To Find a Mockingbird."

17. Lee, *To Kill a Mockingbird*, 89.

18. Joseph Blass, letter to author, 10 September 2002.

19. Ibid.

20. Charles Ray Skinner, interview with author, 22 December 2002.

21. Joseph Blass, letter to author, 10 September 2002.

22. George Thomas Jones, "Courthouse Lawn Was Once Kids' Playground," in *Happenings in Old Monroeville*, vol. 2 (Monroeville, Ala.: Bolton Newspapers, 2003), 163.

23. Lawrence Grobel, *Conversations with Capote* (New York: New American Library, 1985), 53.

24. Rudisill, with Simmons, *Capote*, 191.

25. Betty Martin, interview with author, 5 November 2005. Mrs. Martin, who lived on the outskirts of Monroeville, knew Hattie Clausell.

26. Roberta Steiner, "My Cousin Carson McCullers," Carson McCullers Society Newsletter, no. 3, University of West Florida, Pensacola, Fla., 2000.

27. Thomas Daniel Young, Introduction to Part III in *A History of Southern Literature*, ed. Louis D. Rubin, Jr., et al. (Baton Rouge: Louisiana State University Press, 1985), 262.

28. Marie Faulk Rudisill, interview with author, 21 December 2005.

29. Mary Tucker, interview with Monroe County Heritage Museums, Monroeville, Ala., 7 July 1998.

30. Rudisill, interview with author, 21 December 2005.

31. Grobel, *Conversations with Capote*, 53.

32. Truman Capote, "Christmas Vacation" (1935–36), in Bradford Morrow, ed., *Conjunctions: 31: Radical Shadows: Previously Untranslated and Unpublished Works by 19th and 20th Century Writers* (New York: Bard College, 1998), 142.

33. Freda Roberson Noble, letter to author, 18 September 2002.

34. Rudisill, interview with author, 21 December 2005.

35. Taylor Faircloth, interview with author, 17 March 2003.

36. Lee, *To Kill a Mockingbird*, 81.

37. Gerald Clarke, *Capote: A Biography* (New York: Simon and Schuster, 1988), 22.

38. "Story of Attempted Drowning Called False, Angers Harper Lee," *Tuscaloosa News*, 25 September 1997.

39. Lee, *To Kill a Mockingbird*, 6.

40. Ibid., 77.

Chapter 2: "Apart People"

1. Lee, *To Kill a Mockingbird*, 144.

2. *Monroeville: The Search for Harper Lee's Maycomb* (Charleston, S.C.: Arcadia Publishing, 1999), 26.

3. Ibid., 23.

4. Molly Haskell, "Unmourned Losses, Unsettled Claims" (book review), *The New York Times*, 12 June 1988, 1.

5. Clarke, *Capote: A Biography*, 14.

6. Skinner, interview with author, 22 December 2002.

7. George Thomas Jones, *Happenings in Old Monroeville* (Monroeville, Ala.: Bolton Newspapers, 1999), 126.

8. Rudisill, with Simmons, *Capote*, 193.

9. Jubera, "To Find a Mockingbird."

10. Anne Taylor Fleming, "The Private World of Truman Capote, *New York Times*, 16 July 1978.

11. Patricia Burstein, "Tiny, Yes, but a Terror? Do Not Be Fooled by Truman Capote in Repose," *People*, 10 May 1976, 12–17.

12. Rudisill, with Simmons, *Capote*, 241–42.

13. Eugene Walter (as told to Katherine Clark), *Milking the Moon* (New York: Three Rivers Press, 2001), 40.

14. Gloria Steinem, " 'Go Right Ahead and Ask Me Anything' (And So She Did): An Interview with Truman Capote," *McCall's*, November 1967, 76–77, 148–52, 154.

15. *Monroeville: The Search for Harper Lee's Maycomb*, 70.

16. Burstein, "Tiny, Yes, but a Terror?" 12–17.

17. Lee, *To Kill a Mockingbird*, 18.

18. Roy Newquist, *Counterpoint* (Chicago: Rand McNally, 1964), 407.

19. Marianne M. Moates, *A Bridge of Childhood: Truman Capote's Southern Years* (New York: Henry Holt, 1989), 116.

20. Harper Lee, "A Letter from Harper Lee," *O Magazine*, July 2006, 152.

21. Truman Capote papers, Box 7, folders 11–14, New York Public Library. Nelle begins her notes on the research for Capote's *In Cold Blood*: "These Notes Are Dedicated to the Author of The Fire and the Flame. . . ."

22. Newquist, *Counterpoint*, 407.

23. 1930 *United States Federal Census*, National Archives and Records Administration, T626, 2,667 rolls, Washington, D.C.; also, George Thomas Jones, letter to author, 16 March 2004.

24. Freda Roberson Noble, letter to the author, 18 September 2002; also, Jones, letter to the author, 8 October 2002.

25. Skinner, interview with author.

26. Lee, *To Kill a Mockingbird*, 12.

27. George Plimpton, *Truman Capote: In Which Various Friends, Enemies, Acquaintances, and Detractors Recall His Turbulent Career* (New York: Nan A. Talese, 1997), 14.

28. Truman Capote, *Other Voices, Other Rooms* (1948; reprint, New York: Vintage/Random House, 1994), 132.

Chapter 3: First Hints of *To Kill a Mockingbird*

1. Moates, *A Bridge of Childhood*, 169.

2. Claude Nunnelly, interview with author, 7 December 2003.

3. Jones, "Courthouse Lawn," 140.

4. Freda Roberson Noble, letter to author, 25 April 2003.

5. Sue Philipp, interview with author, 9 March 2004.

6. Freda Roberson Noble, letter to author, 25 April 2003.

7. Ibid.

8. Jubera, "To Find a Mockingbird."

9. Freda Roberson Noble, letter to author, 25 April 2003.

10. Ibid.; also, *Monroeville: The Search for Harper Lee's Maycomb*, 41.

11. Harper Lee, "Springtime," *Monroe Journal*, 1 April 1937.

12. "Harper Lee Began Writing in Childhood, Sister Says," *Alabama Journal*, 20 November 1963.

13. Jubera, "To Find a Mockingbird."

14. Dr. Wanda Bigham, letter to author, 9 April 2004. Dr. Bigham is a former president of Huntingdon College.

15. Vernon Hendrix, "Firm Gives Books to Monroe County," *Montgomery Advertiser,* 23 December 1962.

16. *Journal of the House of Representatives of Alabama,* 1935, House Bill 191, 418–19.

17. Jane Kansas, "To Kill a Mockingbird & Harper Lee: Why the Site?" http://mockingbird.chebucto.org/why.html. Kansas offers hard-to-find anecdotes about the Lees.

18. Alice Lee, speech presented at "Maud McLure Kelly Award Luncheon" (award given to Miss Alice Lee, Mobile, Ala., 18 July 2003).

19. Ibid.

20. Elizabeth Otts, "Lady Lawyers Prepare Homecoming Costumes," *Crimson White,* 26 November 1946, 14.

21. Catherine Helms, letter to author, 14 June 2003.

22. "Tests," *The Huntress* (Huntingdon College), 11 October 1944, 1.

23. Jeanne Foote North, letter to author, 17 February 2003.

24. Ibid.

25. Catherine Helms, letter to author, 18 June 2003.

26. Mary Tomlinson, interview with author, 30 April 2003.

27. Catherine Helms, interview with author, 29 March 2003.

28. Tomlinson, interview with author, 30 April 2003.

29. Tina Rood, letter to author, 16 February 2003.

30. Catherine Helms, letter to author, 20 June 2003.

31. Mary Nxell Atherton, interview with author, 25 February 2003.

32. Harper Lee, "Nightmare," *The Prelude* (Huntingdon College literary magazine) (Spring 1945): 11.

33. Lee, *To Kill a Mockingbird,* 118.

34. Harper Lee, "A Wink at Justice," *The Prelude* (Huntingdon College literary magazine) (Spring 1945): 14–15.

35. Ann Richards Somers, interview with author, 14 March 2003.

36. Florence Moore Stikes, letter to author, 26 April 2003.

Chapter 4: *Rammer Jammer*

1. Barbara Moore, letter to author, 13 December 2003.

2. *The Corolla* 1946 (University of Alabama at Tuscaloosa yearbook), "Chi Omega," 231.

3. Polly Terry, interview with author, 31 January 2003.

4. Mary Anne Berryman, interview with author, 5 February 2003.

5. Jane Benton Davis, interview with author, 8 March 2004.

6. Mary Anne Berryman, letter to author, 3 February 2003.

7. Ibid.

8. Benton Davis, interview with author, 8 March 2004.

9. Moore, letter to author, 13 December 2003.

10. Harper Lee, "Caustic Comment," *Crimson White*, 16 August 1946, 2.

11. Ibid.

12. Mildred H. Jacobs, interview with author, 7 December 2003.

13. John T. Hamner, "This Mockingbird Is a Happy Singer," *Montgomery Advertiser*, 7 October 1960.

14. Lee, "Caustic Comment," 2.

15. Harper Lee, "Alabama Authors Write of Slaves, Women, GIs," *Crimson White*, 1 October 1946, 2.

16. Ernest Maygarden, letter to author, 3 December 2003.

17. Hamner, "Happy Singer."

18. "'Little Nelle' Heads Ram, Maps Lee's Strategy," *Crimson White*, 8 October 1946, 1.

19. Elise Sanguinetti, interview with author, 5 November 2005.

20. Harper Lee, "Now Is the Time for All Good Men" (a one-act play), *Rammer Jammer*, October 1946, 7, 17–18.

21. Winzola McLendon, "Nobody Mocks 'Mockingbird' Author: Sales Are Proof of Pudding," *Washington Post*, 17 November 1960, B12.

22. Carney Dobbs, letter to author, 5 December 2002.

23. Dan Meador, interview with author, 9 March 2004.

24. Mary Lee Stapp, interview with author, 11 March 2004.

25. Jane Williams, interview with author, 12 March 2004.

26. Marion Goode Shirkey, interview with author, 23 January 2003.

27. Olive Landon, interview with author, 16 March 2004.

28. Jane Williams, interview with author, 12 March 2004.

29. "Miss Nelle Lee Chosen to Attend Oxford," *Monroe Journal*, 29 April 1948, 1.

30. Roy E. Hranicky, interview with author, 6 December 2004.

31. "Programme for the 1948 Delegacy for Extra-Mural Studies Summer School: European Civilization in the Twentieth Century." Oxford University Archives (CE 3/384), Bodleian Library, Oxford, England.

32. Marja Mills, "A Life Apart: Harper Lee, The Complex Woman Behind 'A Delicious Mystery,'" *Chicago Tribune*, 13 September 2002.

33. Ibid.

34. John Forney, a fellow University of Alabama alumnus—and, like Nelle, a "Campus Character" in the college yearbook—met Nelle at Penn Station and recounted this anecdote to friends.

Chapter 5: "Willing to Be Lucky"

1. E. B. White, *Here Is New York* (New York: Harper & Brothers, 1949).

2. "Rubbish in Manhattan Streets" (letter to the editor), *New York Times*, 11 May 1949.

3. At the November 8, 1962, Mount Holyoke 125-year anniversary commemoration, Nelle received an honorary doctorate. As part of the ceremony, her bookstore experience was mentioned. Most sketches of her adult life begin with her working at an airline.

4. Maryon Pittman Allen (former U.S. senator from Alabama), letter to author, 30 November 2003.

5. Olga Lee Ryan, letter to author, 22 April 2003.

6. Mills, "A Life Apart."

7. Walter, *Milking the Moon*, 93.

8. Jubera, "To Find a Mockingbird."

9. Harper Lee, "Christmas to Me," *McCall's*, December 1961, 63.

10. Ibid.

11. Ibid.

12. Ibid.

13. Ibid.

14. "Alumna Wins Pulitzer Prize for Distinguished Fiction," University of Alabama *Alumni News* (May–June 1961).

15. Nelle Harper Lee to Leo R. Roberts, 26 January 1960, Archives and Information Center, Huntingdon College Library, Huntingdon Collection.

16. Carter Wilson, interview with author, 19 November 2004. Wilson was one of Tay Hohoff's young authors in the early 1960s.

17. Tay Hohoff, "We Get a New Author," *Literary Guild Book Club Magazine*, August 1960, 3–4.

18. Ibid.

19. *The Author and His Audience*, 175th anniversary J. B. Lippincott. (Philadelphia: J. B. Lippincott, 1967), 28.

20. Ibid.

21. Hohoff, "New Author," 3–4.

22. Newquist, *Counterpoint*, 412.

23. Hazel Rowley, "Mockingbird Country," *The Australian's Review of Books*, April 1999.

24. "Negro Held for Attacking a Woman," *Monroe Journal*, 9 November 1933, 1.

25. 1930 *United States Federal Census*, National Archives and Records Administration, T626, 2,667 rolls, Washington, D.C.

26. *State of Alabama v. Walter Lett*, Monroe County Courthouse, Monroeville, Ala.

27. "Lett Negro Saved from Electric Chair," *Monroe Journal*, 12 July 1934, 1.

28. C. E. Johnson, M.D., to Hon. B. M. Miller, governor, 20 July 1934, Death Cases (Executions, Reprieves and Commutations) by Gov. B. M. Miller, Alabama State Archives, Montgomery, Ala.

29. G. M. Taylor, M.D., to Hon. B. M. Miller, governor, 23 July 1934, Alabama State Archives, Montgomery, Ala.

30. "Negro law," not taught in any law school or codified in any statute book, was a blur that whipped past black defendants. Part show, part legal twaddle, it rested, wrote Southern historian Leon Litwack in *Trouble in Mind*, "largely on custom, racial assumptions, the unquestioned authority of whites, and a heavy dose of paternalism." The tone was set for a case involving a Negro when a judge appointed an attorney for the accused. Usually counsel for the defense was a newly minted lawyer, a beginner like A. C. Lee was in 1919.

31. Lee, *To Kill a Mockingbird*, 5–6.

32. Truman Capote, letter to Alvin and Marie Dewey, 12 August 1960. In Gerald Clarke, ed., *Too Brief a Treat: The Letters of Truman Capote* (New York: Random House, 2004), 290.

33. Capote, letter to Alvin Dewey III, 4 July 1964, in Clarke, ed., *Too Brief*, 401.

34. Lee, *To Kill a Mockingbird*, 6.

35. Phoebe Adams, Review of *To Kill a Mockingbird*, by Harper Lee, *The Atlantic Monthly*, August 1960, 98–99.

36. "Harper Lee," *Contemporary Authors Online*, Gale, 2004. Reproduced in *Biography Resource Center*, Farmington Hills, Mich.: The Gale Group, 2004.

37. W. J. Stuckey, *The Pulitzer Prize Novels: A Critical Backward Look* (Norman: University of Oklahoma Press, 1966), 194.

38. "Harper Lee Gets Scroll, Tells of Book," *Birmingham News*, 12 November 1961.

39. Hal Boyle, "Harper Lee Running Scared, Getting Fat on Heels of Success," *Birmingham News*, 15 March 1963.

40. *The Author and His Audience*, 29.

41. Sue Philipp, interview with author, 9 March 2004.

42. *The Author and His Audience*, 28.

43. McLendon, "Nobody Mocks 'Mockingbird' Author," B12.

44. *The Author and His Audience*, 28.

45. Dr. Grady H. Nunn, letter to author, 1 December 2003.

46. *The Author and His Audience*, 29.

47. Kay Anderson, letter to author, 15 March 2004. As a student at Monroe County High School, Anderson heard Harper Lee tell the story of throwing the manuscript out the window, which Alice Lee denied. Several other former students heard the same story over the years. The "for better or for worse" remark is from Newquist, *Counterpoint*, 405.

48. Sarah Countryman, interview with author, 9 March 2004.

49. *Monroeville: The Search for Harper Lee's Maycomb*, 44.

50. "Wealthy Farmer, 3 of Family Slain," 16 November 1959, *New York Times*, 7.

51. Clarke, *Capote: A Biography*, 319.

Chapter 6: "See NL's Notes"

1. George Plimpton, "The Story Behind a Nonfiction Novel," 16 January 1966, *New York Times*, http://nytimes.com/books/97/12/28/home/capote-interview.html.

2. Capote papers, New York Public Library, Manuscripts and Archives

Division, box 7, folders 11–14. These folders contained dated but not numbered typewritten notes by Harper Lee.

3. Alvin A. Dewey, as told to Dolores Hope, "The Clutter Case: 25 Years Later KBI Agent Recounts Holcomb Tragedy," *Garden City Telegram*, 10 November 1984, compact disc.

4. Dewey, in Hope, *Garden City*, ibid.

5. Ibid.

6. Ibid.

7. Ibid.

8. Clarke, *Capote: A Biography*, 322.

9. Harold Nye, interview with author, 30 December 2002.

10. "Scene of the Crime: Twenty-Five Years Later, Holcomb, Kansas, Remembers 'In Cold Blood.'" *Chicago Sunday Tribune*, 11 November 1984, 33.

11. "Scene of the Crime," *Chicago Sunday Tribune*, 11 November 1984, 33.

12. Capote papers, New York Public Library, box 7, folders 11–14, 26 December 1959.

13. Clarke, *Capote: A Biography*, 323.

14. Cliff Hope, interview with author, 5 April 2005.

15. Ibid.

16. Holly Hope, *Garden City: Dreams in a Kansas Town* (Norman: University of Oklahoma Press, 1988), 61.

17. Dewey, in Hope, "The Clutter Case."

18. Dolores Hope, letter to author, 8 June 2005.

19. Plimpton, "The Story Behind a Nonfiction Novel."

20. Holly Hope, interview with author, 17 February 2005.

21. Harold Nye, interview with author, 30 December 2002.

22. Capote papers, New York Public Library, box 7, folder 8. Folder 8 contains some of Capote's notes.

23. Dewey, in Hope, "The Clutter Case."

24. Plimpton, *Truman Capote: In Which Various Friends*.

25. Capote papers, New York Public Library, box 7, folder 8.

26. Ibid., folders 11–14; 11 January 1960.

27. Capote papers, Library of Congress, box 4, Ac 14, 421; 11 January 1960.

28. Capote papers, New York Public Library, box 7, folders 11–14; 11 January 1960.

29. Ibid.

30. Ibid.

31. Ibid.

32. Ibid.

33. Ibid.

34. Newquist, *Counterpoint*, 407.

35. Truman Capote, letter to Cecil Beaton, 21 January 1960. In Clarke, *Too Brief a Treat*, 276–77.

36. Elon Torrence, interview with author, 6 May 2005. Mr. Torrence is a former Associated Press reporter who attended the trial.

37. Capote papers, New York Public Library, box 7, folders 11–14, 22 March 1960.

38. Ibid., 19 March 1960.

39. Elon Torrence, interview with author, 6 May 2005.

40. "America's Worst Crime in Twenty Years," Richard Eugene Hickock, as told to Mack Nations, *Male*, December 1961, 30–31, 76–83.

41. Capote papers, New York Public Library, box 7, folders 11–14, (no date).

42. Mark Besten, "Too Hot for You? Take a Dip in Cold Blood," *Louisville Eccentric Observer*, 1 August 2001, 16.

Chapter 7: *Mockingbird* Takes Off

1. Capote, letter to David O. Selznick and Jennifer Jones, early June 1960, in Clarke, *Too Brief a Treat*, 284.

2. Newquist, *Counterpoint*, 407.

3. Untitled item, *Monroe Journal*, 16 June 1960.

4. Glendy Culligan, "Listen to That Mockingbird," *Washington Post*, 3 July 1960, E6.

5. Frank H. Lyell, "Violence in Dixie" (review) *Seed in the Wind*, by Leon Odell, *New York Times*, 31 July 1960, BR23.

6. Capote, letter to Alvin and Marie Dewey, 10 October 1960, in Clarke, *Too Brief a Treat*, 299.

7. "Mocking Bird Call," *Newsweek*, 9 January 1961, 83.

8. Tay Hohoff, *Cats and Other People* (New York: Popular Library, 1973), 195.

9. Max York, "Throngs Greet Monroe Writer," *Montgomery Advertiser,* 13 September 1960.

10. Vernon Hendrix, "Author's Father Proud of 'Mockingbird' Fame," *Montgomery Advertiser,* 7 August 1960.

11. Capote, letter to Andrew Lyndon, 6 September 1960, in Clarke, *Too Brief a Treat,* 291.

12. Albin Krebs, "Truman Capote Is Dead at 59; Novelist of Style and Clarity," *New York Times,* 28 August 1984.

13. "Mocking Bird Call," 83.

14. Ibid.

15. Ibid.

16. Unsigned letter to Harper Lee from a secretary in Williams's office, 7 January 1961, Annie Laurie Williams papers, Columbia University, box 86.

17. Charles Ray Skinner, interview with author, 22 December 2002.

18. Nelle Harper Lee to Leo R. Roberts, 26 January 1960, Archives and Information Center, Huntingdon College Library, Huntingdon Collection.

19. Frances Kiernan, "No Apologies Necessary," *The Atlantic Monthly,* April 2001.

20. Hendrix, "Author's Father Proud."

21. Emma Foy, interview with author, 5 July 2003.

22. Annie Laurie Williams to Nelle and Alice Lee, 28 January 1961, Williams papers, box 86.

23. "Mockingbird Film May Begin in Fall," *Birmingham News,* 2 May 1961.

24. "Spreading Poison" (letter to the editor), *Atlanta Journal,* 7 February 1961.

25. Annie Laurie Williams to George Stevens with note attached from Harper Lee, 8 August 1960, Williams papers, box 86.

26. Maurice Crain to Alice Lee, 22 March 1961, Williams papers, box 86.

27. Murray Schumach, "Prize for Novel Elates Film Pair," *New York Times,* 19 May 1961, 26.

28. "State Pulitzer Prize Winner Too Busy to Write," *Dothan Eagle,* 2 May 1961.

29. " 'Luckiest Person in the World.' "

30. "Mocking Bird Call," 83.

31. Truman Capote, letter to Alvin and Marie Dewey, 22 May 1961, in Clarke, *Too Brief a Treat,* 317.

32. Nelle Lee to Helen McGowin, 20 November 1961, Caldwell Delaney papers, University of South Alabama Archives.

33. Note to Harper Lee, 12 July 1961, Williams papers, box 86.

34. "'Luckiest Person in the World.'"

Chapter 8: "Oh, Mr. Peck!"

1. Reed Polk, letter to author, 10 July 2003.

2. Scott McGee, Kerryn Sherrod, and Jeff Stafford, "To Kill a Mockingbird: The Essentials," Turner Classic Movies, www.turnerclassicmovies.com.

3. Joseph Deitch, "Harper Lee: Novelist of the South," *Christian Science Monitor*, 3 October 1961, 6.

4. Charles S. Watson, *Horton Foote: A Literary Biography* (Austin: University of Texas Press, 2003), 114. Nelle didn't quite feel "indifference," as she claimed. In a letter to Helen McGowin, a friend in Mobile, dated November 20, 1961, Nelle wrote: "Please forgive the long silence from Monroeville. I had to do some things that HAD to be done as soon as I returned—the most pressing task was doctoring the movie script" (Caldwell Delaney papers, University of South Alabama).

5. Don Noble, *Bookmark: Interview with Horton Foote*, videocassette, Alabama Center for Public Television, Tuscaloosa, Ala., 27 August 1998.

6. *To Kill a Mockingbird: Then and Now*, videocassette, Prince William County Public Schools, Manassas, Va., 25 April 1997.

7. M. Jerry Weiss, "To Kill a Mockingbird," *Photoplay Guide*, NCTE Studies in the Mass Media (Champaign, Ill.: National Council of Teachers of English, March 1963), 18.

8. *To Kill a Mockingbird*, Commentary section, Universal City, Calif.: Universal Home Video, 1998, compact disc.

9. Williams to George Stevens, 23 May 1961, Annie Laurie Williams papers, Rare Book and Manuscript Library, Columbia University, box 86.

10. Gary Fishgall, *Gregory Peck: A Biography* (New York: Scribner, 2002), 233.

11. George Thomas Jones, "Stand Up, Monroeville, Gregory Peck Is Passin'." *Happenings in Old Monroeville*, vol. 2 (Monroeville, Ala.: Bolton Newspapers, 2003), 159–60.

12. Ibid., 160–61.

13. Dolores Hope, letter to author, 15 October 2002.
14. Thomas McDonald, "Bird in Hand," *New York Times*, 6 May 1962, 149.
15. Kansas, "To Kill a Mockingbird & Harper Lee: Why the Site?"
16. "Brock Peters, 'To Kill a Mockingbird' Actor, Dies at 78," *USA Today*, 23 August 2005.
17. *To Kill a Mockingbird*, Commentary section, compact disc.
18. Barbara Vancheri, "Author Lauded 'Mockingbird' as a 'Moving' Film," *Pittsburgh Post-Gazette*, 20 February 2003.
19. Philip Alford, interview with author, 21 May 2004.
20. Murray Schumach, "Film Crew Saves $75,000 on Shacks," *New York Times*, 19 January 1962, 26.
21. Newquist, *Counterpoint*, 406.
22. Kansas, "To Kill a Mockingbird & Harper Lee: Why the Site?"
23. Alford, interview with author, 21 May 2004.
24. Ibid.
25. Vernon Hendrix, "Firm Gives Books to Monroe County," *Montgomery Advertiser*, 23 December 1962.
26. A. C. Lee, "This Is My Father's World," Bounds Law Library, University of Alabama at Tuscaloosa.
27. A. B. Blass, "Mockingbird Tales," *Legacy* (magazine of the Monroe County Heritage Museums), Fall/Winter 1999, 22.
28. Ramona Allison, "'Mockingbird' Author Is Alabama's 'Woman of the Year,'" *Birmingham Post Herald*, 3 January 1962.
29. Lee, *To Kill a Mockingbird*, 30.
30. Reverend Thomas L. Butts, Remarks at "Maud McLure Kelly Award Luncheon," (award given to Miss Alice Lee, Mobile, Ala., 18 July 2003).
31. E.L.H., Jr., "The Obvious Is All Around Us" (editorial), *Birmingham News*, 22 April 1962.
32. Truman Capote, letter to Alvin and Marie Dewey, 5 May 1962, in Clarke, *Too Brief a Treat*, 348.
33. Fishgall, *Gregory Peck*, 236.
34. Ibid.
35. *To Kill a Mockingbird*, Commentary section, compact disc.
36. Truman Capote, letter to Alvin and Marie Dewey, 16 August 1962, in Clarke, *Too Brief a Treat*, 361.
37. Truman Capote, letter to Donald Cullivan, 11 December 1962, in Clarke, *Too Brief a Treat*, 372.

38. "Author Praises Picture Made from Prize Novel," *New York Times*, Williams papers (a clipping in Harper Lee's file).

39. *To Kill a Mockingbird*, Commentary section, compact disc.

40. *Newsweek*, 18 February 1963, 93.

41. Bosley Crowther, "Screen: 'To Kill a Mockingbird.'" *New York Times*, 15 February 1963, 10.

42. Colin Nicholson, "Hollywood and Race: *To Kill a Mockingbird*," in *Cinema and Fiction: New Modes of Adapting, 1950–1990*, eds. John Orr and Colin Nicholson (Edinburgh, Scotland: Edinburgh University Press, 1992), 97.

43. M. Jerry Weiss, "To Kill a Mockingbird," *Photoplay Guide*, 18.

44. Dorothy and Taylor Faircloth, interview with author, 17 March 2003.

45. Joseph Blass, letter to author, 10 September 2002.

46. Dorothy and Taylor Faircloth, interview with author, 17 March 2003.

47. S. Jonathan Bass, *Blessed Are the Peacemakers: Martin Luther King, Jr., Eight White Religious Leaders, and the "Letter from Birmingham Jail"* (Baton Rouge: Louisiana State University Press, 2001), 102–103.

48. Vernon Hendrix, "Harper Lee Cries for Joy at Peck's Winning of Oscar," *Montgomery Advertiser*, 10 April 1963.

49. Moates, *A Bridge of Childhood*, 11.

Chapter 9: The Second Novel

1. Amelia Young, "Her Writing Place Is Secret: 'Mockingbird' Author Working on Second Book," *Minneapolis Star*(?), 26 May 1963, Williams papers, box 86. (The clipping is barely identifiable.)

2. Wes Lawrence, "Author's Problem: Friends," *Cleveland Plain Dealer*, 17 March 1964.

3. James B. Simpson, *Simpson's Contemporary Quotations* (New York: Houghton Mifflin, 1988).

4. Hal Boyle, "Harper Lee Running Scared, Getting Fat on Heels of Success," *Birmingham News*, 15 March 1963.

5. Joseph Deitch, "Harper Lee: Novelist of the South," *Christian Science Monitor*, 3 October 1961, 6.

6. Alice Lee to Annie Laurie Williams, 14 November 1963, Williams papers, box 86.

7. Young, "Her Writing Place Is Secret."

8. Ibid.

9. Truman Capote, letter to Bennett Cerf, 10 September 1962, in Clarke, *Too Brief a Treat*, 363.

10. Harold Nye to Capote, 27 June 1962, Capote papers, New York Public Library, box 7, folder 9.

11. Harold Nye, interview with author, 30 December 2002.

12. Newquist, *Counterpoint*, 407–12.

13. Ibid.

14. Truman Capote, letter to Perry Smith, 24 January 1965, in Clarke, *Too Brief a Treat*, 412.

15. Brig. Gen. Jack Capp (Ret.), letter to author, 1 July 2006.

16. Ibid.

17. Gus Lee, *Honor and Duty* (reprint, New York: Ivy Books, 1994), 149–50.

18. Ibid.

19. Clarke, *Capote: A Biography*, 354.

20. Don Lee Keith, "An Afternoon with Harper Lee," *Delta Review* (Spring 1966).

21. Williams to Alice Lee, 5 August 1965, Williams papers, box 86.

22. Lee, "When Children Discover America," 76–79.

23. Wayne Lee, "Emotions Mixed Among Clutter Participants," *Hutchinson News*, 31 October 1965.

24. Williams to Alice Lee, 28 September 1965, Williams papers, box 86.

25. Sarah Countryman, interview with author, 9 March 2004.

26. Williams to Alice Lee, 8 October 1965, Williams papers, box 86.

27. Wayne Greenhaw, letter to author, 1 November 2005.

28. R. Philip Hanes, interview with author, 6 December 2004.

29. Michael Shelden, "The Writer Vanishes: The 36-Year Silence of Harper Lee," *Daily Telegraph*, 12 April 1997.

30. David Kipen, letter to author, 23 November 2005. Mr. Kipen is the National Endowment for the Arts literature director.

31. Wayne Greenhaw, interview with author, 20 March 2004.

32. Peter Griffiths, letter to the author, 26 April 2005. Mr. Griffiths was a researcher for the BBC in 1982, which visited Monroeville for a documentary about *To Kill a Mockingbird*.

Chapter 10: Quiet Time

1. Tom Radney, interview with author, 14 November 2005.
2. Jubera, "To Find a Mockingbird."
3. Tom Radney, interview with author, 14 November 2005.
4. Ralph Hammond, interview with author, 20 March 2005.
5. Burstein, "Tiny, Yes, but a Terror?"
6. James Wolcott, "Tru Grit," *Vanity Fair*, October 2005, 166.
7. Tom Radney, interview with author, 14 November 2005.
8. Ibid.
9. Drew Jubera, "'Mockingbird' Still Sings Despite Silence of Author Harper Lee," *Atlanta Journal-Constitution*, 26 August 1990, M1 and M3.
10. William Smart, interview with author, 2 July 2004.
11. Clarke, *Capote: A Biography*, 22.
12. Harper Lee to Caldwell Delaney, 30 December 1988. Robert Hicks, author of *Widow of the South* (New York: Warner Books, 2005), came upon this letter in a used copy of Clarke's *Capote: A Biography*.
13. *Monroeville: The Search for Harper Lee's Maycomb*, 86.
14. Christopher Sergel to Annie Laurie Williams, 5 January 1965, Williams papers, box 149, folder L.
15. "Harper Lee, Read but Not Heard," *Washington Post*, 17 August 1990.
16. Roy Hoffman, "Long Lives the Mockingbird," *New York Times*, 9 August 1998.
17. Kathy McCoy, letter to author, 11 August 2004.
18. Dr. Wanda Bigham, former president of Huntingdon College, letter to author, 25 May 2004.
19. George Thomas Jones, letter to author, 30 August 2003.
20. Mills, "A Life Apart."
21. Ibid.
22. J. Wes Yoder, "Debating the Details: Some Residents of Monroeville Prefer to Ponder the Fine Points of Famous Novel," *Expressions* (online magazine), Auburn University Journalism Department, 2001.
23. Mills, "A Life Apart."
24. Kathy Kemp, "Mockingbird Won't Sing," *News & Observer*, 12 November 1997, E1.

25. Mary Tomlinson, letter to author, 2 November 2005.

26. Carla Jean Whitley, "Small-Town Q&A: Amanda McMillan." *Crimson White*, University of Alabama at Tuscaloosa, 9 October 2003.

27. Don Collins, interview with author, 1 April 2004.

28. Alice Lee, "92nd Birthday Newsletter," 22 September 2003.

29. Mills, "A Life Apart."

30. Carolyn Crawford, interview with author, 1 February 2003.

31. "One Version of the Harper Lee Story," Harper Lee listserv at www.yahoogroups.com, 11 October 2005.

32. Nelle Lee to Helen McGowin, 20 November 1961, Caldwell Delaney papers, University of South Alabama Archives.

Bibliography

Books

The Author and His Audience. 175th Anniversary J. B. Lippincott. Philadelphia: J. B. Lippincott, 1967.

Ayers, Edward L. *The Promise of the New South: Life After Reconstruction.* New York: Oxford University Press, 1992.

Bloom, Harold, ed. *To Kill A Mockingbird: Modern Critical Interpretations.* Philadelphia: Chelsea House Books, 1999.

Capote, Truman. *In Cold Blood.* 1965. Reprint, New York: Vintage, 1994.

——. *Other Voices, Other Rooms.* 1948. Reprint, New York: Vintage, 1994.

Centennial Edition of *The Monroe Journal.* Monroeville, Ala.: *Monroe Journal,* December 22, 1966.

Clarke, Gerald. *Capote: A Biography.* New York: Simon and Schuster, 1988.

——, ed. *Too Brief a Treat: The Letters of Truman Capote.* New York: Random House, 2004.

Collins, Donald E. *When the Church Bell Rang Racist: The Methodist Church and the Civil Rights Movement in Alabama.* Macon, Ga.: Mercer University Press, 1998.

Fishgall, Gary. *Gregory Peck: A Biography.* New York: Scribner, 2002.

Greenhaw, Wayne. "Capote Country." *Alabama on My Mind.* Montgomery, Ala.: Sycamore Press, 1987.

Grobel, Lawrence. *Conversations with Capote.* New York: New American Library, 1985.

Hohoff, Tay. *Cats and Other People.* New York: Popular Library, 1973.

Holt, Dan. *Kansas Bureau of Investigation, 1939–1989.* Marceline, Mo.: Jostens, 1990.

Hope, Holly. *Garden City: Dreams in a Kansas Town.* Norman: University of Oklahoma Press, 1988.

Inge, Thomas M. *Truman Capote Conversations.* Jackson: University of Mississippi Press, 1987.

Johnson, Claudia Durst. *To Kill a Mockingbird: Threatening Boundaries.* New
   York: Twayne, 1994.

Jones, George Thomas. *Happenings in Old Monroeville.* Monroeville, Ala.:
   Bolton Newspapers, 1999.

———. *Happenings in Old Monroeville.* Volume 2. Monroeville, Ala.: Bolton
   Newspapers, 2003.

Lee, Harper. *To Kill a Mockingbird.* 1960. Reprint, New York: Warner Books,
   1982.

Litwack, Leon F. *Trouble in Mind: Black Southerners in the Age of Jim Crow.*
   New York: Alfred A. Knopf, 1998.

Moates, Marianne M. *A Bridge of Childhood: Truman Capote's Southern Years.*
   New York: Henry Holt, 1989.

Monroeville: Literary Capital of Alabama. Charleston, S.C.: Arcadia Publishing,
   1998.

Monroeville: The Search for Harper Lee's Maycomb. Charleston, S.C.: Arcadia
   Publishing, 1999.

Moore, Albert Burton, ed. *History of Alabama and Her People.* 3 vols. Chicago:
   American Historical Society, 1927.

Morrow, Bradford and Peter Constantine, eds. *Conjunctions: 31: Radical
   Shadows: Previously Untranslated and Unpublished Works by 19th and 20th
   Century Masters.* New York: Bard College, 1998.

Nance, William L. *The Worlds of Truman Capote.* New York: Stein and Day,
   1970.

Newquist, Roy. *Counterpoint.* Chicago: Rand McNally, 1964.

Nicholson, Colin. "Hollywood and Race: *To Kill a Mockingbird.*" In *Cinema
   and Fiction: New Modes of Adapting, 1950–1990.* John Orr and Colin
   Nicholson, eds. Edinburgh, Scotland: Edinburgh University Press, 1992.

O'Neill, Terry, ed. *Readings on* To Kill A Mockingbird. San Diego:
   Greenhaven Press, 2000.

Plimpton, George. *Truman Capote: In Which Various Friends, Enemies,
   Acquaintances and Detractors Recall His Turbulent Career.* New York:
   Nan A. Talese, 1997.

Rubin, Louis D., Jr., et al., eds. *A History of Southern Literature.* Baton Rouge:
   Louisiana State University Press, 1985.

Rudisill, Marie, with James C. Simmons. *Truman Capote: The Story of His
   Bizarre and Exotic Childhood by an Aunt Who Helped Raise Him.* New York:
   William Morrow, 1983.

Stuckey, W. J. *The Pulitzer Prize Novels: A Critical Backward Look*. Norman: University of Oklahoma Press, 1966.

Walter, Eugene (as told to Katherine Clark). *Milking the Moon*. New York: Three Rivers Press, 2001.

Watson, Charles S. *Horton Foote: A Literary Biography*. Austin: University of Texas Press, 2003.

White, E. B. *Here Is New York*. New York: Harper & Brothers, 1949.

Articles

Adams, J. Donald. Speaking of Books (column). *New York Times*, 2 June 1963, 270.

Adams, Phoebe. Review of *To Kill a Mockingbird* by Harper Lee. *The Atlantic Monthly*, August 1960, 98–99.

Allison, Ramona. " 'Mockingbird' Author Is Alabama's 'Woman of the Year.' " *Birmingham Post Herald*, 3 January 1962.

"Alumna Wins Pulitzer Prize for Distinguished Fiction." University of Alabama *Alumni News* (May–June 1961).

"America's Worst Crime in Twenty Years." Richard Eugene Hickock as told to Mack Nations. *Male*, December 1961.

"Annie L. Williams, Authors' Agent, Dies." *New York Times*, 18 May 1977, O4.

"Annie Williams, Agent Who Sold 'Gone With the Wind.' " *Washington Post*, 20 May 1977, C8.

Bass, S. Jonathan. *Blessed Are the Peacemakers: Martin Luther King, Jr., Eight White Religious Leaders, and the "Letter from Birmingham Jail."* Baton Rouge: Louisiana State University Press, 2001.

Besten, Mark. "Too Hot for You? Take a Dip in Cold Blood." *Louisville Eccentric Observer*, 1 August 2001, 16.

Blass, A. B. "Mockingbird Tales." *Legacy* (magazine of the Monroe County Heritage Museums). (Fall/Winter 1999): 22.

Boyle, Hal. "Harper Lee Running Scared, Getting Fat on Heels of Success." *Birmingham News*, 15 March 1963.

Brian, Denis. "Truman Capote." In *Truman Capote Conversations*. Thomas M. Inge, ed. Jackson: Mississippi, 1987, 210–235.

"Brock Peters, 'To Kill a Mockingbird' Actor, Dies at 78." *USA Today*, 23 August 2005.

Buder, Leonard. "Opportunities for Study in Europe." *New York Times,* 11 April 1948, E11.

Burstein, Patricia. "Tiny, Yes, but a Terror? Do Not Be Fooled by Truman Capote in Repose." *People,* 10 May 1976, 12–17.

Capote, Truman. "The Thanksgiving Visitor." In *A Christmas Memory, One Christmas, & The Thanksgiving Visitor.* New York: Modern Library, 1996.

"Christopher Sergel, Publisher of Plays and Playwright, 75." *New York Times,* 12 May 1993, B7.

Cobb, Mark Hughes. "Native Stars Fall on Alabama Hall of Fame." *Tuscaloosa News,* 17 March 2001.

Crowther, Bosley. "Screen: 'To Kill a Mockingbird.' " *New York Times,* 15 February 1963.

Culligan, Glendy. "Listen to That Mockingbird." *Washington Post,* 3 July 1960, E6.

Curtis, Charlotte. "Capote's Black & White Ball: 'The Most Exquisite of Spectator Sports.' " *New York Times,* 29 November 1966, 53.

Dare, Tim. "Lawyers, Ethics, and *To Kill a Mockingbird.*" *Philosophy and Literature* 25 (April 2001): 127–41.

Deitch, Joseph. "Harper Lee: Novelist of the South." *Christian Science Monitor,* 3 October 1961, 6.

E. L. H., Jr. "The Obvious Is All Around Us." *Birmingham News,* 22 April 1962.

Erisman, Fred. "The Romantic Regionalism of Harper Lee." *Alabama Review* 26 (1973): 122–36.

"Exchange Students Sail: But Only 105 Leave on Marine Jumper Under U.S. Plan." *New York Times,* 7 June 1947, 29.

Feeney, F. X. "A Tale of Three Parties: Recalling Truman Capote." In George Plimpton, ed. *Truman Capote: In Which Various Friends, Enemies, Acquaintances and Detractors Recall His Turbulent Career. LA Weekly,* 13–20 February 1998.

"1st Novel Wins Pulitzer Prize." *Washington Post,* 12 May 1961, A3.

Going, William T. "Truman Capote: Harper Lee's Fictional Portrait of the Artist as an Alabama Child." *Alabama Review* 42, no. 2 (April 1989): 136–49.

Greenhaw, Wayne. "Capote Country." In *Alabama on My Mind.* Montgomery, Ala.: Sycamore Press, 1987.

Hamner, John T. "This Mockingbird Is a Happy Singer." *Montgomery Advertiser,* 7 October 1960.

"Harper Lee Gets Scroll, Tells of Book." *Birmingham News*, 12 November
   1961.

"Harper Lee, Read but Not Heard." *Washington Post*, 17 August 1990.

Hendrix, Vernon. "Author's Father Proud of 'Mockingbird' Fame."
   Montgomery Advertiser, 7 August 1960.

———. "Firm Gives Books to Monroe County." *Montgomery Advertiser*,
   23 December 1962.

———. "Harper Lee Cries for Joy at Peck's Winning of Oscar." *Montgomery
   Advertiser*, 10 April 1963.

Hodges, Sam. "To Love a Mockingbird." *Mobile Register*, 8 September 2002.

Hoff, Timothy. "Influences on Harper Lee: An Introduction to the
   Symposium." *Alabama Law Review* 45 (Winter 1994): 389.

Hoffman, Roy. "Long Lives the Mockingbird." *New York Times Book Review*,
   9 August 1998, 31.

Hohoff, Tay. "We Get a New Author." *Literary Guild Book Club Magazine*,
   August 1960, 3–4.

"John Megna, 42, 'Mockingbird' Star" (obit). *New York Times*, 7 September
   1995, B17.

Johnson, Claudia Durst. "The Secret Courts of Men's Hearts: Code and Law
   in Harper Lee's *To Kill a Mockingbird*." *Studies in American Fiction* 19
   (Autumn 1991): 129–39.

Jones, George Thomas. "Courthouse Lawn Was Once Kids' Playground." In
   Happenings in Old Monroeville. Vol. 2. Monroeville, Ala.: Bolton
   Newspapers, 2003.

———. "Stand Up, Monroeville, Gregory Peck Is Passin'." *Happenings in Old
   Monroeville*. Vol. 2. Monroeville, Ala.: Bolton Newspapers, 2003, 159–60.

———. "Young Harper Lee's Affinity for Fighting." EducETH.ch (The
   English Page), 7 December 1999, <www.educeth.ch/english/readinglist/
   leeh/remin.html#fight>.

Jubera, Drew. "'Mockingbird' Still Sings Despite Silence of Author Harper
   Lee." *Atlanta Journal-Constitution*, 26 August 1990, M1 and M3.

———. "To Find a Mockingbird." *Dallas Times Herald*, 1984.

Keith, Don Lee. "An Afternoon with Harper Lee." *Delta Review* (Spring
   1966): 40–41, 75, 81–82.

Kemp, Kathy. "Mockingbird Won't Sing." *News & Observer*, 12 November
   1997, E1.

Krebs, Albin. "Truman Capote Is Dead at 59; Novelist of Style and Clarity."
   New York Times, 28 August 1984.

Lawrence, Wes. "Author's Problem: Friends." *Cleveland Plain Dealer,* 17 March 1964.

Lee, Gus. *Honor and Duty.* Reprint. New York: Ivy Books, 1994.

Lee, Harper. "Alabama Authors Write of Slaves, Women, GIs." *Crimson White,* 1 October 1946, 2.

———. "Caustic Comment." *Crimson White,* 28 June 1946, 2.

———. "Christmas to Me." *McCall's,* December 1961, 63.

———. Foreword to the 35th anniversary edition of *To Kill a Mockingbird.* New York: HarperCollins, 1993.

———. "Nightmare." *The Prelude* (Huntingdon College literary magazine), 11.

———. "Now Is the Time for All Good Men" (one-act play). *Rammer Jammer,* October 1946, 7, 17–18.

———. "Some Writers of Our Times." *Rammer Jammer,* November 1945, 14.

———. "Springtime." *Monroe Journal,* 1 April 1937, 3.

———. "A Wink at Justice." *The Prelude* (Huntingdon College literary magazine), 14–15.

Lee, Wayne. "Emotions Mixed Among Clutter Participants." *Hutchinson News,* 31 October 1965.

"Lett Negro Saved from Electric Chair." *Monroe Journal,* 12 July 1934, 1.

Letter to the editor. "Caustic Comment." *Crimson White,* 2 August 1946, 2.

Letter to the editor. "Spreading Poison." *Atlanta Journal,* 7 February 1961.

" 'Little Nelle' Heads Ram, Maps Lee's Strategy." *Crimson White,* 8 October 1946, 1.

Lubet, Steven. "Reconstructing Atticus Finch." *Michigan Law Review* 97 no. 6 (1999): 1339–62.

" 'Luckiest Person in the World,' Says Pulitzer Winner." *Birmingham News,* 2 May 1961.

McCoy, Kathy. "*To Kill a Mockingbird:* The Great American Novel." *Legacy* (Monroe County Heritage Museums), 1994, 22–25.

McDonald, Thomas. "Bird in Hand." *New York Times,* 6 May 1962, 149.

McGee, Scott, Kerryn Sherrod, and Jeff Stafford. *To Kill a Mockingbird: The Essentials.* Turner Classic Movies, www.turnerclassicmovies.com

McLendon, Winzola. "Nobody Mocks 'Mockingbird' Author: Sales Are Proof of Pudding." *Washington Post,* 17 November 1960, B12.

Mills, Marja. "A Life Apart: Harper Lee, The Complex Woman Behind 'A Delicious Mystery.' " *Chicago Tribune,* 13 September 2002.

"Miss Nelle Lee Chosen to Attend Oxford." *Monroe Journal,* 29 April 1948, 1.

Mitgang, Herbert. "Books of the Times" (column). *New York Times*, 13 July 1960, 33.

"Mocking Bird Call." *Newsweek*, 9 January 1961.

"Mockingbird Film May Begin in Fall." *Birmingham News*, 2 May 1961.

"Negro Held for Attacking a Woman." *Monroe Journal*, 9 November 1933, 1.

"Nelle Harper Lee." In Charles Moritz, ed. *Current Biography*. New York: H. W. Wilson Co., 1961.

Nicholson, Colin. "Hollywood and Race: *To Kill a Mockingbird*." In John Orr and Colin Nicholson, eds. *Cinema and Fiction: New Modes of Adapting, 1950–1990*. (Edinburgh, Scotland: Edinburgh University Press, 1992), 97.

"One Version of the Harper Lee Story." www.yahoogroups.com (listserv), 11 October 2005.

Otts, Elizabeth. "Lady Lawyers Prepare Homecoming Costumes." *Crimson White*, 26 November 1946, 14.

Park, Mary Jane. "Truman's Aunt Tiny." *St. Petersburg Times*, 3 October 2000, www.sptimes.com/News/100300/Floridian/ Truman_s_Aunt_Tiny.shtml.

Pennypacker, Nathaniel. "Massacre of the Clutter Family." *Front Page Detective*, April 1960.

Plimpton, George. "The Story Behind a Nonfiction Novel." *New York Times*, 16 January 1966, <http://nytimes.com/books/97/12/28/home/ capote-interview.html.

"Prize Winner Remembered as Deflater of Phoniness." *Montgomery Advertiser*, 4 May 1961.

Rhodes, Matthew W. "Truman Capote." *Legacy* (Monroe County Heritage Museums), 1994, 26–31.

Romine, Dannye. "Truman's Aunt: A Bio in Cold Blood." *Chicago Tribune*, 5 June 1983, sec. 5, 1–2.

Rowley, Hazel. "Mockingbird Country." *The Australian's Review of Books*, April 1999.

"Scene of the Crime: Twenty-Five Years Later, Holcomb, Kansas Remembers 'In Cold Blood.'" *Chicago Sunday Tribune*, 11 November 1984.

Schumach, Murray. "Film Crew Saves $75,000 on Shacks." *New York Times*, 19 January 1962, 26.

———. "Prize for Novel Elates Film Pair." *New York Times*, 19 May 1961.

Shackelford, Dean. "The Female Voice in *To Kill a Mockingbird*: Narrative Strategies in Film and the Novel." In Harold Bloom, ed., *To Kill a*

Mockingbird: Modern Critical Interpretations. Philadelphia: Chelsea House, 1999, 121.

"State Pulitzer Prize Winner Too Busy to Write." *Dothan Eagle,* 2 May 1961.

Steinem, Gloria. "'Go Right Ahead and Ask Me Anything' (And So She Did): An Interview with Truman Capote." *McCall's,* November 1967, 76–77, 148–52, 154.

Steiner, George. "A Cold-Blooded Happening." *Guardian,* 2 December 1965.

"Story of Attempted Drowning Called False, Angers Harper Lee." *Tuscaloosa News,* 25 September 1997.

"Tay Hohoff, Author, Lippincott Officer" (obit). *New York Times,* 12 January 1974, 36.

"They All Had a Ball at Capote's Party." *Washington Post,* 30 November 1966, D2.

"Traffic Ticket Report." *Saturday Review,* 6 August 1960.

Vancheri, Barbara. "Author Lauded 'Mockingbird' as a 'Moving' Film." *Pittsburgh Post-Gazette,* 20 February 2003.

"Wealthy Farmer, 3 of Family Slain." *New York Times,* 16 November 1959, 7.

Weiler, A. H. "New Midtown Showcase—Other Film Matters." ("Bird" Team.) "By Way of Report" (column). *New York Times,* 29 January 1961, X7.

Weiss, M. Jerry. "To Kill a Mockingbird." *Photoplay Guide.* NCTE Studies in the Mass Media. Champaign, Ill.: The National Council of Teachers of English, March 1963, 18.

Whitley, Carla Jean. "Small-Town Q&A: Amanda McMillan." *Crimson White,* University of Alabama at Tuscaloosa, 9 October 2003.

Wiebe, Crystal K. "Author Left Mark on State." LJ [*Lawrence Journal*] World.com, 3 April 2005.

———. "'To Kill a Mockingbird' Author Helped Truman Capote Break the Ice in Kansas." LJ [*Lawrence Journal*]World.com, 3 April 2005.

Wolcott, James. "Tru Grit." *Vanity Fair,* October 2005.

Woodard, Calvin. "Listening to the Mockingbird." *Alabama Law Review* 45 (Winter 1994): 563–85.

Yoder, J. Wes. "Debating the Details: Some Residents of Monroeville Prefer to Ponder the Fine Points of Famous Novel." *Expressions* (online magazine). Auburn University Journalism Department, 2001.

York, Max. "Throngs Greet Monroe Writer." *Montgomery Advertiser,* 13 September 1960.

Young, Amelia. "Her Writing Place Is Secret: 'Mockingbird' Author Working on Second Book." *Minneapolis Star* (?), 26 May 1963.

Young, Thomas Daniel. Introduction to Part III in *A History of Southern Literature*. Louis D. Rubin, Jr., et al, eds. Baton Rouge: Louisiana State University Press, 1985, 262.

Zoerink, Richard. "Truman Capote Talks About His Crowd." *Playgirl*, September 1975, 50–51, 54, 80–81, 128.

Media

Dewey, Alvin A., as told to Dolores Hope. "The Clutter Case: 25 Years Later KBI Agent Recounts Holcomb Tragedy." *Garden City Telegram*, 10 November 1984, compact disc.

Noble, Don. "Bookmark: Interview with Horton Foote." Videocassette. Alabama Center for Public Television. Tuscaloosa, Ala., 27 August 1998.

To Kill a Mockingbird. CD. Commentary section. Universal City, Calif.: Universal Home Video, 1998.

" 'To Kill a Mockingbird': Then and Now." Videocassette. Prince William County Public Schools. Manassas, Va., 25 April 1997.

Index

(Page references in *italic* refer to illustrations.)